A LITTLE
GAY
HISTORY
OF
WALES

D1513957

A LITTLE GAY HISTORY OF WALES

DARYL LEEWORTHY

UNIVERSITY OF WALES PRESS

2019

www.uwp.co.uk

British Library Cataloguing-in-Publication Data
A catalogue record for this book is available from the British Library.

ISBN   978-1-78683-480-5
eISBN   978-1-78683-481-2

The right of Daryl Leeworthy to be identified as author of this work has been asserted in accordance with sections 77 and 79 of the Copyright, Designs and Patents Act 1988.

The University of Wales Press acknowledges the financial support of the Welsh Books Council.

Typeseting and layout by Marie Doherty
Printed by CPI Antony Rowe, Melksham

For Rhian, David and Christian.
It's one thing to see, it's another to understand.

Contents

Abbreviations
ix
Preamble
xi

PART I: COMING OUT
Chapter One: Hidden From View?
3
Chapter Two: Legal Limitations
23

PART II: COMING TOGETHER
Chapter Three: Seeking Love, Finding It
43
Chapter Four: Dancing the Night Away
67

PART III: CHANGING THE WORLD
Chapter Five: Law Reform and Afterwards
87
Chapter Six: A Lost World?
115

Acknowledgements
139
Select Bibliography
143
Index
155

Abbreviations

BP	*Bad Press*
CHE	Campaign for Homosexual Equality
CLS	Cardiff Local Studies and Heritage Library, Cathays
CT	*Cardiff Times*
CYLCH	Cymdeithas y Lesbaid a Hoywon Cymraeg eu Hiaith
DT	*Double Take*
EEx	*Evening Express*
FRIEND	Fellowship for the Relief of the Isolated and Emotionally in Need and Distress
GA	Glamorgan Archives, Cardiff
GLF	Gay Liberation Front
GN	*Gay News*
GR	*Gair Rhydd*
LAGNA	Lesbian and Gay Newsmedia Archive, Bishopsgate Institute, London
LCLGR	Labour Campaign for Lesbian and Gay Rights
LGBT	Lesbian, Gay, Bisexual and Transgender
LGSM	Lesbians and Gays Support the Miners
NLW	National Library of Wales, Aberystwyth
NUM	National Union of Mineworkers
NUPE	National Union of Public Employees.

NUS	National Union of Students
PG	*Police Gazette*
SWA	*South Wales Argus*
SWDN	*South Wales Daily News*
SWDP	*South Wales Daily Post*
SWE	*South Wales Echo*
SWEP	*South Wales Evening Post*
UCC	University College Cardiff
UCNW	University College of North Wales, Bangor
UCS	University College Swansea
WM	*Western Mail*

Preamble

On the last Friday of October 1984, a group of lesbians and gay men travelled from London to the Dulais Valley. The following day the group were guests of honour at a social in Onllwyn Welfare Hall organised by the Neath, Dulais and Swansea Valleys Miners' Support Group. One of them, a working-class Liverpudlian, got up on stage and gave a short speech explaining who they were, and how and why they had raised the money donated a few weeks before. At the end of the night, as Rod Stewart's hit song *Sailing* played, couples gay and straight danced together in what was later regarded as a turning-point. A few weeks afterwards, Mike Jackson, the group's secretary, reflected on the journey and the experiences he had had: the trip 'was one of the happiest moments of my life', he wrote, 'and I'm sure I speak for everyone in our group who also had the honour of staying with you.' Others agreed that it was 'one of the most moving experiences of all our lives'.[1]

When the story of Lesbians and Gays Support the Miners (LGSM) was told in Stephen Beresford's 2014 film *Pride,* some of the surviving participants described it as a romance. Siân James told an audience at Big Pit in Blaenafon that the film was about 'two communities that fell in love with each other'.[2] It was never certain either side would generate such warm feelings; indeed some in the gay community in London were adamant that the miners deserved no support. 'How many of them [LGSM] have lived in a mining community', wrote one correspondent in July 1984, 'I would say not or they would know of the ignorance and false machismo.'[3] Dai Donovan similarly remembered in 1986 that he

> was very nervous when the lesbians and gays came down because I sort of realised how nervous they were and how people down here would react to them, but it was outstanding you know. For the first time they came to a community [where] they were able to live as ordinary members of the community, go to an ordinary club and dance with each other, which is something they couldn't do even in London.

Donovan first met with LGSM outside Paddington Station in September 1984. He was there to collect a cheque for five hundred pounds, which LGSM were donating. In discussion with LGSM, Donovan came to recognise that working-class lesbians and gays were being exploited even in a place where they ostensibly had the greatest freedom of all. 'They were', he observed, 'as much prisoners in London as they had been in their own communities ... [it was a] very sad life in a way.' Recognition of the situation carried forward to the support group in Onllwyn, challenging their perceptions of gay life in the capital and paving the way for mutual understanding.

LGSM likewise had their eyes opened to local conditions. Writing in the gay magazine *Square Peg*, one member of the group pondered life as it 'must have been' in the coalfield: 'repressive [and] being the brunt of anti-gay jokes if you ever found the courage to come out'.[4] By the time the Pits and Perverts benefit gig at the Camden Electric Ballroom was held in December 1984, the bond between LGSM and the Dulais Valley was very strong indeed. So much so that teenagers from the area were encouraged to go to the concert. There was no outward sense of division and little sign of hostility. It was at Pits and Perverts that Dai Donovan made his now famous 'You have worn our badge' speech alongside Hefina Headon, the support group's secretary, who announced the belated arrival of women's liberation to Onllwyn. 'We had no idea of the power we had', she declared, 'that will not be suppressed. We will never go back to sitting at home.'[5]

Dozens of miners from the South Wales Area of the NUM and their families joined the gay pride march through London in the summer of 1985; it was a symbolic gesture towards intercommunity solidarity. Not only was this the first pride march to feature non-gay people; it was perhaps the largest contingent of Welsh men and women that had yet taken part in gay pride events in the capital.[6] As the *Valleys Star*, the support group's newsletter, observed:

> Last Saturday, June 29, saw a drawing together of the links made by our support group with the Lesbian and Gay Committee in London. Over forty people from this area joined with ten thousand gays and lesbians in their annual Gay Pride March through the streets of London. It was a tremendous feeling to be in Hyde Park listening to the cheers when the support group and lodge banners were raised.

Although LGSM was the largest of the lesbian and gay support groups which emerged during the strike, it was by no means the only link between gay liberation and the industrial struggle in the coalfield. A lesbian and gay group from Southampton joined forces with the NUM lodge in Abercynon and recalled later that

> Our best personal experiences were meeting miners who came to the city from Abercynon. After coming down here repeatedly and meeting politically active socialists, seeing them collect money, food and clothing, and generally working in support of the strikers, their attitudes were forced to change just by their own experiences, because they know we are just ordinary people, and people who support their struggle.[7]

An LGSM group was also established in Cardiff, and members of the Labour Campaign for Lesbian and Gay Rights living in Swansea and Bristol were active in providing support for the miners through wider networks, although these others had none of the impact in much larger communities that LGSM had in small ones.

LGSM's story was – and is – an inspirational one and it provided a fillip for local activism for several years after the strike: during lesbian and gay awareness week at University College Cardiff in February 1987, *All Out! Dancing in Dulais*, the documentary made by LGSM, was shown at the student union.[8] But it was all too easy to imagine that the events of 1984–5 marked a sudden departure in the advance of lesbian and gay rights. They did not. Instead, a light was shone on a form of political campaigning that had been marginal to mainstream politics, to be sure, but never entirely absent. The dynamo of what I have elsewhere called Labour Country had been social democratic politics based on material equality and articulated in a language of class; but this fell away in the aftermath of the miners' strike, and into the vacuum came the politics of identity. That is, the politics of gender, sexuality, race, and, most especially, national identity and language.

Something of these tensions can be found in a series of films which appeared in the early 1990s and embraced the subject of gay life in a way never previously attempted, at least in Wales. Whereas 'for many years Welsh people [had] been forced to see themselves on screen as often uninformed visiting film crews [had] seen them', the advances of this period ensured that the camera's gaze steadily became more 'inside-looking-out' than the other way around. It was a gaze more attuned to the margins of contemporary life, too.[9]

Gadael Lenin (Leaving Lenin), a hurried production filmed over the course of five weeks on location in early post-Soviet St Petersburg, first alerted audiences to this new environment. Written by Siôn Eirian and directed by Endaf Emlyn, the film addressed artistic fealty, personal loyalties and teenage sexuality with remarkable sensitivity, avoiding the pitfalls of parody, melodrama, camp and the over-comedic. One of its central characters, Spike, a rebellious sixth former tormented by personal tragedy, slowly emerged from a fog of sadness to fall in love with a free-spirited young Russian artist called Sascha. In an important scene filmed on Trinity Bridge (then Kirov Bridge), Spike came out to his art teacher begging her to be released from conformity.

It was a brave step forward. Attitudes towards homosexuality had worsened considerably in the second half of the 1980s, partly because of the AIDS crisis but also because of the conservative values inculcated by the Thatcher government and its allies in the media. In 1987, attitudes to gay people reached a nadir with three-quarters of those questioned by the British Social Attitudes

Survey stating that homosexual relationships were mostly or always wrong. A mere 11 per cent felt they were never wrong – a figure that had been nearly twenty per cent at the start of the decade. Although these numbers began steadily to improve, even by the mid-1990s, when *Gadael Lenin* was being shown in cinemas, under half of those born in the 1970s (that is, who were in or approaching their twenties) regarded homosexuality as 'not wrong at all'. And for the most part, popular culture was silent about non-heterosexual relationships. Those gay and lesbian voices heard on television and radio, in film, in the theatre or in literature, rarely had a Welsh accent; and, even then, lived far away. *Gadael Lenin* was a landmark.

In 1996, *Gadael Lenin* was followed by one of the stand-out works of late-twentieth-century Welsh language television, *Bydd yn Wrol* (Courage, Brother). This one-off drama told a story of post-industrial decline in the Valleys, a common theme at the time, but amidst the parochial squabbles and the potential demise of the local workmen's hall, a symbol of older struggles and political imaginations, there was a profound consideration of generational conflict and teenage concern about sexualities. The plural was essential. The lead character, played sensitively by Matthew Rhys in his break-out role, steadily came to the realisation of his homosexuality. He was guided through that process by an older resident, Henry George, played by Islwyn Morris. 'I want to thank him publicly', the young man says, in a funeral oration for the latter, 'for showing me how to be brave. It takes a strong, good man to show someone else the way. And because of Henry George, I can be proud of what I am today.'[10]

Bydd yn Wrol also followed on from the more disturbing *Dafydd* produced by the BBC for its Wales Playhouse series in 1995. Starring Richard Harrington, *Dafydd* transposed two queer men, again from the Valleys, from Llandeilo in the western extremity of the former coalfield, and Pontypridd in its centre, to the gritty streets of Amsterdam where hustling, crime and dishonesty were the order of the day. Focused on the marginalisation of gay men, this was a programme permeated with considerations of social class and an awareness of Valleys culture not easily reducible to stereotypes: the lead character chooses classical music to listen to over dance and techno, then more prevalent in nightclubs or gay bars, and enthusiastically attends the opera, much to the amusement and bemusement of his working-class Dutch friends, who view it as distinctly bourgeois and not for the likes of them.

Each of the films presented gay life in the 1990s in distinct ways: alienation from the Valleys, accommodation in the Valleys, the dangers of sex, the uncertainties of affection, and the complex processes of coming out (or not). In their varying approaches they depicted a community that, despite progress and change, remained very much unsure of itself – if it could be described as a community at all. And this contingency had always been present for those individuals now so often grouped together under the acronym LGBT (lesbian, gay, bisexual and transgender). It was notable that each of the films dealt either with Valleys culture or with people from the southern coalfield. This reflected the regionalised nature of gay activism and social life: there was no national campaign group until the early twenty-first century, no national newsletter either, and there was a sharp divergence between southern and northern attitudes particularly, amongst local government bodies and agencies of the state.[11]

But how to begin constructing – even reconstructing – a social and cultural history of the Welsh past attuned to the experiences and lives of ordinary gay men and women? What sort of language might be used? What period should be focused on? Did distinct Welsh traditions develop? When serious histories of sexuality were first written in the 1970s the emphasis was on recovery of a history useful to the gay liberation movement. Recently the stress has been on the fluid nature of sexuality and desire challenging artificial boundaries between 'straight' and 'gay' in favour of the 'disruptive' character of the 'queer'. In place of homosexuality came queerness and same-sex desire, and in place of a chronology of progress from criminalisation to expanding freedoms, came more contingent narratives full of fragment and uncertainty. A kaleidoscope, then, rather than a telescope. Queer historians have tended to stress class differences in the experience of sexuality since working- and middle-class Britons were 'generally different – both materially and emotionally'.[12]

The proponents of queer history have sought to move the discussion on from politics, activism and nineteenth-century legal and medical discourse to consider everyday lives, 'queer cultures' and representations. They have sought, in other words, to unpick and understand the experiences of those portrayed by the police, the courts and the press in the following manner:

> At Bow Street Police Court on Thursday, Mr Garrett passed a sentence of six months' imprisonment with hard labour on Sidney Harold Leech (26), dancer, of St John's Road, Brixton, for importuning army officers in Pall Mall East for immoral purposes. When arrested the prisoner had his face powdered, his lips rouged, and his eyelids pencilled. A powder puff was found in his pocket. He denied the charge, and said that he had been in receipt of 29s a week unemployment since July last. He served in the army for more than two years, and was discharged in December 1917 as medically unfit.[13]

This article, appearing on the front page of Swansea's *South Wales Weekly Post* in October 1919, provides an indication of the types of evidence used by queer historians to demonstrate that 'there was no Gay London, either in 1885 or in 1914. Rather, there were men from various walks of life, some who would have recognized the others, some who would not' and thus there can be no clear identification in the past of a singular sexual identity – sexuality itself is called into question. A variety of terms are used by queer historians to convey aspects of 'queer experience' – same-sex desire, homosex, homosocial, even 'twilight moments' – all with a view to avoiding a binary between 'normal' and 'abnormal' or heterosexual and homosexual, since, in the words of Helen Smith, 'there was no sexual normal to set them against', at least until some time after the Second World War.[14]

This book is informed by both traditions: it accepts the stress on fluidity and disruption posed by queer history for the period before the Second World War, but in turn reasserts the role of political activism and liberation movements. In short, it traces the steady, but always contingent, emergence of gay public cultures, which was itself a response to the decline of a homosocial world centred on the workplace and other collective social environments. For this was not a story of unfolding progress, a great march towards a queer utopia, but one of advance and decline of both civil rights and social attitudes, and, above all, opportunities for self-expression and identification. Welsh men and women took their full part in the struggle to progress civil rights, but they were also part of the negative social and cultural reaction. Each theme ran as counterpoint to the other, and these two aspects of the past, of support and opposition, provide our social, cultural and political dynamics. Likewise, where an individual lived mattered quite as much as *how* they lived. South Wales was often less hostile than the north. Thus in 1990, an individual living with AIDS in Criccieth felt they had to leave their home because of prejudice and victimisation. They moved to England.[15]

It was a familiar story. Time and again, the social and cultural atmosphere in many parts of Wales seemed inimical to living lives differently from the norm, and the migrant's trail took away those who felt oppressed. And when they did not move away to the large urban centres of England, they came to settle in Cardiff. Of necessity, the city dominates any history of gay Wales: it had the most visible community, the most accessible infrastructure, and in various forms since the late 1960s has been able to sustain a public gay culture.[16]

Although such visibility was not entirely new, and the busy docklands of Cardiff had always had their fair share of cruising, it was the commercialism of the 1960s that encouraged a different kind of 'scene'. In the past, it had helped that part of the population was transient and social habits were in flux. On the one hand, ships arrived from abroad, offloaded their cargo, and for a while their crews remained in port seeking creature comforts; and on the other, visitors travelled into the city from the Valleys and further afield with business and pleasure in mind. Sex, alcohol and narcotics were readily available, and sailors and other visitors regularly found themselves in court for having sought relief in the right-wrong sorts of places. Newspapers, hardly immune to salacious gossip about the dark side of life in port, particularly when it meant increased sales, nevertheless adopted hushed tones and carefully circumscribed the details provided about 'unnatural offences' committed in and around the docks, in railway underpasses, in parks, in public toilets and in the back of taxis. As the Chief Constable of Cardiff complained in 1938,

When horse-drawn hackney carriages plied for hire in this city their drivers were frequently penalised for allowing their vehicles to be used ... for immoral purposes. Taxicabs took their place and, for a time, some of their drivers were guilty of the same practices. Today, taxicabs are comparatively few in number, but it is a common sight to see supposedly respectable men driving private motor cars, soliciting prostitutes and other immoral women to enter their cars and proceed to unfrequented places for immoral purposes. A trail of disease and misery is frequently the aftermath of these nocturnal excursions.[17]

It is not outside the boundaries of possibility that such situations also involved men cruising other men.

The more journalists, the police and the courts involved themselves in the attempt to control these kinds of activities, the more they developed a private portfolio of terms used to attribute homosexuality to persons of interest, with provincial police forces taking the lead from the Metropolitan Police. Identification often had no surer grounds than observed assumption, and the glossary went far beyond with whom a person had sex. The police kept an eye out for those who dressed flamboyantly, whose mannerisms deviated from those which were, at the time, expected of a man or a woman, they noted how a person spoke, and with whom they kept company. Gossip, too, functioned as a social commentary about 'confirmed bachelors' or lifelong spinsters or friends who never married but who were 'close companions' for much of their life. Official habits were not always shared by the general population, and this helps to explain why some had little sense of marginalisation and others felt alienated.

Negative sentiments and a desire to ameliorate were what motivated the legal reform movement of the 1950s and 1960s and gave some impetus to the liberation movements of the 1970s. What occurred in the late 1960s with the changing of the legal proscription of homosexuality was thus not accidental but the result of grassroots activism, shifting public mood and a growing recognition particularly within the Labour Party of the need to deal with social and cultural as well as material conditions. The key figure was Roy Jenkins, Monmouthshire-born and Cardiff-educated, who, as Home Secretary in the mid-1960s and again in the 1970s, liberalised criminal justice, censorship and race relations, and encouraged and enabled the private members' bills which led to the decriminalisation of abortion and the partial decriminalisation of homosexuality. He was also keen to equalise the age of consent.

Jenkins first wrote about equality and social egalitarianism in the early 1950s during the vigorous debates between the two primary factions within the Labour Party about its future direction: the Bevanites and the Gaitskellites. As a committed Gaitskellite, Jenkins understood equality to mean equality of opportunity quite as much as the permissive society for which he was later vilified by conservatives. During his tenure as Home Secretary, he used the Home Office as a vehicle for these ideas. In this way he became a 'beneficent sympathiser' of homosexual law reform.[18] Together with the arts ministry established under the leadership of Jennie Lee, these changes aimed at contrasting the modern world 'against the drabness, uniformity and joylessness of much of the social furniture we have inherited from the industrial revolution', and in so doing 'making Britain a gayer and more cultivated country'.[19]

Partial decriminalisation in 1967 was steered through Parliament by Leo Abse (in the Commons) and Lord Arran (in the upper chamber). Born into a Jewish family of cinema operators in Cardiff in 1917, Leo Abse had spent the 1930s at the heart of radical politics in the city, even travelling to Spain in 1939 just as the civil war was coming to an end. After service in the Royal Air Force during the Second World War, he settled into legal practice in Cardiff, rose through the ranks of the city's Labour Party becoming chairman in 1951, and was elected to the city council in 1953. In 1958 he succeeded Granville West as the Labour Member of Parliament for Pontypool. With his experience as a solicitor to guide him, Abse focused his attention on improving the legal system and correcting what he regarded as unnecessary and hypocritical intolerance. His 1963 Matrimonial Clauses Act, for instance, simplified the processes by which divorce could be granted.

Abse's first Sexual Offences Bill was tabled in the House of Commons in the autumn of 1961 with the parliamentary debate held on 9 March 1962.[20] Its purpose was not to decriminalise homosexuality, even partially, but to make sentencing more lenient and to prevent 'the witch-hunting which had been shown by the Wolfenden Report to have existed, and which was known by many honourable members to be in existence'. Widespread imprisonment of those found guilty of homosexual offences, he said, forthrightly, was 'about as effective as sending a rapist to the women's prison at Holloway'. Debate on Abse's reform lasted less than an hour before it was adjourned and the bill was eventually abandoned as a lost cause; the attitude of the House of Commons was not then amenable to even a modest reappraisal of the situation. When Abse gained a further opportunity to bring about change in 1966, he seized it, taking the opportunity to go further than had been previously possible. Speaking on the BBC in December 1966, he asserted the simple reasons for changing the law:

> It is not a criminal offence to commit adultery. It is not a
> criminal offence to fornicate. These are not criminal offences
> according to our law, but the fact that the House of Commons
> does not make these criminal offences does not mean that
> we approve of them. And we do not condone homosexuality,
> what the House of Commons has decided is the homosexual
> has enough troubles without in addition having the fear and
> insecurity and the blackmail that arises from the existing law.

Abse frequently returned to this idea in parliamentary debates
on his legislation.

In later years, however, Abse grew ever more frustrated
with segregation and the bifurcation of society into gay and
straight, which he regarded as partly the result of lesbians and
gay men not wanting to integrate into 'mainstream' society. As
he explained to the pioneering documentary film *We Who Have
Friends* in 1969, his concern was now that segregation was an
active choice on the part of the minority, rather than the legalised,
uneducated prejudice of the majority.

> I know it may be a rather, heroic demand, almost, upon
> them, to say to them now look do not retreat into a ghetto.
> We have altered the law so that in fact you need not be as
> replete with fear and anxiety as you had cause to be before.
> And, we say to them therefore that we altered the law because
> we wanted the homosexual could be integrated into the
> wider community. And if you come now with a request or
> a demand that you should have your own clubs, that you
> should in fact create yourselves your own segregation, this
> is bound to cause some misgivings on the part of many of
> us who hoped that just as we could educate the community

to receive the homosexual, so the homosexual could perhaps emancipate himself from his paranoia, from his persecutory feelings, and perhaps come into the community.

The 1967 reforms were undoubtedly a benchmark, which set England and Wales on the road towards tolerance, with social attitudes framed not by criminalisation of sexual activity – although the 1967 legislation was imperfect in that regard – but by education and collective endeavour. In other words, by civil rights. As Abse put it in 1969, the change in the law had led to emancipation from punitive treatment of those who diverged from society's normative values. Equality of outcome had been achieved and the uneven character of the law had been reformed. But there were those, such as Roy Jenkins, who wanted to go further, who believed in equality as an end, rather than a means to an end. Indeed, as Home Secretary in the 1970s, Jenkins sought to improve the earlier legislation by gathering support and evidence in favour of lowering the homosexual age of consent from twenty one, as it had been fixed in 1967, to at least eighteen. The heterosexual age of consent at that time was sixteen. Jenkins knew that there was relatively wide support for a reduction to eighteen, if not equalisation at sixteen, and had this change in mind. As the British Medical Association explained in 1976,

We acknowledge that a lowering to eighteen of the age of consent for men to homosexual acts in private would be reasonable. This would correspond to the legal age of majority. The age of consent would still vary two years as between men and women, but the age of eighteen for men would reflect, in general, their slower rate of biological development.[21]

But it was not to be. By the time the commission appointed by Jenkins in 1976 reported on consent in 1979, the Labour government had fallen. Mrs Thatcher's Conservatives were not in favour of any reduction whatsoever in the homosexual age of consent, and it was not reduced to eighteen until 1994. Full equality did not occur until the year 2000.

My purpose in this book is to establish an LGBT history of Wales 'from below' and to recover something of the lives of those who, with some exercise of caution, can be regarded as having expressed some form of same-sex desire or campaigned for the advancement of civil rights. What readers will possess, then, is a history of both empowerment in a political sense and of social and cultural lives lived regardless of legal constraints. There are a few caveats: it is not my aim to provide a total history, nor have I focused any attention on those, such as the Ladies of Llangollen, Amy Dillwyn, or Evan Morgan, Viscount Tredegar, whose lives were already privileged by wealth and status and who cannot be considered representative of the societies in which they lived, let alone that section of society now characterised as LGBT. Class provides one distinction, gender another. The politics of gay identity embraced by men were less frequently the enthusiasm of women who organised their struggles in different ways – through the women's movement, for instance, or through institutions such as women's aid, women's centres and lesbian lines.

In this way there was never a single community, but many, each with its own dynamics and outlook, community services and possibilities for meeting others; each intersected in different ways by gender, class, and race. This has had a not inconsiderable impact on the surviving archival material used. Much of it can be regarded as ephemeral: adverts, lonely hearts columns, news broadcasts, articles in magazines or student newspapers, and the extant records of campaign groups, together with the material legacies of criminalisation, local government and healthcare services. The individuals who emerged from these records, indicative as inevitably they are, offered clear insight into the historical experiences of gay men and lesbians (in that order), and into men and women who desired other men and women who cannot be accommodated by such labels, but rather less about the experiences of bisexuals and transgender men and women – in the case of the latter until very late in the twentieth century. These contours will be observed in the pages that follow.

Much of what is described took place in a political landscape and, to a lesser extent, a social and cultural environment which was either liberal or social democratic in form. To examine the history of LGBT experience is, then, to hold up a mirror to a place that has traditionally prided itself on radical politics, at least of an economic kind, and to look critically at the presumed social conservatism of communities which embraced social democracy, the Labour Party and the labour movement most completely; to ask questions such as whether Welsh reformers including Leo Abse were operating in a framework of social justice rooted in the communities they represented, rather than striking out entirely independently. It is my view that LGBT history has far more in common with social history and labour history than is often supposed, and the instincts of those forms of writing about the past inform the approach I have adopted: the active recovery of the margins and of the marginalised. LGBT history sheds light on the margins-within-margins and holds to account the promises made by political activists of a more equal society. By addressing questions of gender and sexuality alongside class, we gain a much stronger sense of the past and the ways in which it was experienced in personal terms.

To put it another way: most of those prosecuted by the state for expressing same-sex desire, even in a fleeting moment, perhaps just once, were working-class. They fought on picket lines, struggled to survive during strikes and economic downturns, and lived difficult lives far removed from the material comforts of aristocrats or industrialists. What did it mean to be a miner or a steelworker locked out because, like your comrades, you refused to accept lower wages and worsened conditions, but unlike them you happened to be gay? What difference did your sexuality, known or unknown, make to friends and colleagues? Oftentimes the answer to such questions was simply: it doesn't matter. Yet since the advent of the liberation movement in the 1970s there has been a conscious push by activists to ensure that diversity is understood and known about, historically and contemporaneously, and that oppression is challenged. Writing history is one mechanism to do just that. Indeed, as Deirdre Beddoe argued of women's history, 'without a knowledge of the past, we are always having to begin again.'[22]

A Little Gay History of Wales is, by no means, a tale of endless progress, a turn from the darkness of some unenlightened past of criminalisation and gaol to the more hopeful present of equal marriage and anti-discrimination legislation. The past has always been more complicated than that. The civil rights and freedoms won since the end of the 1960s were the result of a struggle: to come out, to come together, and to change the world. That struggle continues. This is the story of how it came about.

Notes

1. Polly Vittorini, Nicola Field and Caron Methol, 'Lesbians against pit closures', in Vicky Seddon (ed.), *The Cutting Edge: Women and the Pit Strike* (London, 1986), p. 144.

2. Notes in author's possession.

3. *Capital Gay*, 24 July 1984.

4. *Square Peg* (December 1984), 12–13.

5. *Capital Gay*, 14 December 1984.

6. CHE Cardiff, Newsletter, July and August 1980; *Morning Star*, 26 June 1985.

7. Labour Research Department, *Solidarity with the Miners* (London, 1985), p. 29.

8. *GR*, 4 February 1987.

9. David Berry, *Wales and the Cinema: The First Hundred Years* (Cardiff, 1994), p. 11.

10. NLW, MS ex 2827, 'Sgript *Bydd yn Wrol*'.

11. The Welsh-language group CYLCH, which was based in Aberystwyth, had branches elsewhere including Cardiff. See: *Y Ddraig Binc* 3 (Summer 1993); M. Nobbs, 'Queer and Welsh: Double the Trouble', *Rouge* 16 (1994), 22–3; David Bell and Gill Valentine, 'Queer Country: Rural Lesbian and Gay Lives', *Journal of Rural Studies* 11, no. 2 (1995), 113–122. CYLCH is described briefly by Roni Crwydren, 'Welsh lesbian feminist: a contradiction in terms?', in Jane Aaron (ed.), *Our Sisters' Land* (Cardiff, 1994), pp. 299–300.

12. Helen Smith, *Masculinity, Class and Same-Sex Desire in Industrial England, 1895–1957* (London, 2015), p. 7.

13. *South Wales Weekly Post*, 11 October 1919.

14. Smith, *Masculinity*, p. 9.

15. NLW, HTV Wales Archive: News Material, 8 February 1990; NLW, S4C Station Log Collection: Y Byd Ar Bedwar, 4 June 1990.

16. A. P. M. Coxon, *Between the Sheets: Sexual Diaries and Gay Men's Sex in the Era of AIDS* (London, 1996), p. 6.

17. Cardiff City Police, *Annual Report of the Chief Constable for 1938*, p. 9.

18. *Birmingham Daily Post*, 4 July 1967.

19. Lawrence Black, 'Making Britain a Gayer and More Cultivated Country: Wilson, Lee, and the Creative Industries in the 1960s', *Contemporary British History* 20/3 (2006), 324.

20. Parliamentary Archives, Sexual Offences Bill, 1962, HL/PO/PU/2/143.

21. Cited in Matthew Waites, *The Age of Consent: Young People, Sexuality and Citizenship* (London, 2005), p. 134.

22. Deirdre Beddoe, *Discovering Women's History: A Practical Guide to Researching the Lives of Women since 1800* (London, 1998), p. 3.

PART I

Coming Out

CHAPTER ONE

Hidden from View?

Tom Davies was born in 1899. His father, Benjamin Davies, was the minister at Caersalem Baptist Chapel in Abergwynfi and a prominent figure in the local temperance movement.[1] His mother, Elizabeth, shared in the Nonconformist faith. Tom, on the other hand, frequently rebelled, sneaking next door to 'drink eleven years of age' with an older neighbour for whom he used to fetch beer from the off-licence. In May 1914, Tom left school and went to work in the drapery department of Glyncorrwg Co-operative Stores where he revelled in the opportunity to work with fabrics and contemporary fashion. A few months later, life in the Afan Valley was disrupted by war. Although too young to officially join the army, Tom was excited by an advert he saw in the newspaper calling for performers to join the entertainment corps: 'So I told dad, "Dad, I'm going to write away now to London", I said ... and my father said, "don't be so silly" "Yes I am", I said'. Tom was invited to London to audition in singing and dancing and was given a place in the unit.

Tom trained with the noted instructor John Tiller at his school of dancing in London, where he learned high kicks, tap dancing, and how to do the splits. He could already sing very

well, 'I had a lovely voice, and really nicer than Vera Lynn, nicer
than that'. Once he was finished with Tiller's regimen, Tom
joined the YMCA-funded Concert Party led by the actress and
women's suffrage campaigner Lena Ashwell. The first concerts
were held in France early in 1915 – almost forty of them in a
fortnight – but Tom found them too serious for his tastes and
yearned to move on to something less formal where he could
'work a bit of patter [into] my show'. He soon found himself
in concert parties such as *The Duds* in areas such as Arras and
Dieppe before moving on to work with *The Bohemians* at the
Number 14 convalescent depot in Deauville, Normandy. There
he became a member of the entertainment corps troupe based at
the Casino Municipal in neighbouring Trouville-sur-Mer. Other
shows took place in Paris and at the hospital in Saint-Pol-sur-Mer.
As Tom recalled Saint-Pol

> was the first hospital from the line and I was told I would
> have to give a show in one of the wards. Well the men were in
> such agony and groaning and in pain. I said to the ... fellow
> that was running our show there and I said, I can never go
> in, sir, it is breaking my heart to see them, I said ... you didn't
> know what shape they were in you know because everyone
> was covered in a blanket up to here.

Tom's show involved dancing on stage and signing popular wartime songs such as *Keep an Eye on Tommy*, the lyrics of which
Tom clearly understood for their suggestive alterity:

> Sergeant Brown, Sergeant Brown keep an eye on Tommy
>   for me,

> He might go wrong on the contin-nound, when he reaches
> Paree,
> He'll to parlez-vous, they always do, when the French girls
> they see,
> But if my Tommy wants to parlez vous, let him come home
> and parlez vous with me.

Without describing Tom's stage costumery, none of this would seem at all unusual, it was straight out of the musical hall tradition. But Tom took to the stage in elaborate women's costumes offering risqué routines that maintained a sense of mystery as to his gender:

> I'd come out in this beautiful sequin gown you know, and then I used to take my gown off, and I had sequin briefs and a sequin bra, and I was naked then but for my tights. And I had these two big ostrich feather fans, and I had learned to manipulate them ... they wouldn't see anything, and I could hear them saying, Jock, how would you like her in the bunk tonight ....
>
> There were many who wouldn't believe I was male, you know, because I was so dainty. And a funny thing whatever frock came from London I didn't have to have it altered at all. I had a small waist.

Tom's stage persona was Peggy Deauville. With a high, effeminate voice and slight frame, he readily passed for a woman and encouraged catcalls and wolf whistling from the all-male audience. On several occasions, Tom explained, 'absolute filth' was shouted at the stage:

> I remember I was with Lew Stone, and he and I had a sketch
> that was very popular, and so now, there was a bedroom scene
> you see, so he'd pull me round and he'd throw me back on
> the bed, you see, and I'd fall in the most suggestive way like,
> you know, with this beautiful nightdress and all that on you
> know, and he'd go to the front of the stage ... and say, 'what
> can I do, I love this woman, I love this woman, what can I
> do'. And a voice at the back shouted, 'oh for heaven's sake',
> he said, 'get into bed with her', he said, 'get stuck into her
> and let's get on with the show'.

After the war, Tom stayed on in Paris working in a variety of
theatres, including the *Folies Bergères*. He began impersonating
prominent contemporary figures such as the nurse Edith Cavell
and actress Gaby Deslys and began attracting the attention of
French magazines for his habit of travelling around the country
in drag. He was photographed 'wearing the conventional Pierrot
costume with frilled collar and black pom-pom buttons but with
the addition of high-heeled shoes and black net stockings and
surrounded by a squadron of amused and admiring soldiers'.[2]
For a period Tom worked in Germany and after returning to
Britain spent six years working for Bud Flanagan as a dancer
and performer in the Victoria Palace and the London Palladium.
By 1939, he had settled back in Blaengwynfi and worked once
again for Glyncorrwg Co-op. After the war, he performed at
British Legion clubs and other working-class venues in the
Valleys.

In oral testimony, Tom never mentioned isolation or ostracism from the wider community for his performances, although
this might have been different had he walked the streets of
Glyncorrwg in drag as he walked the streets of Paris.[3] For him

the Valleys were accepting and embracing, and his father did not try to intervene even though as chapel minister he was regarded as a guardian of contemporary moral values. As Tom put it,

Oh Glyncorrwg people all of them knew me. Well they know me now because they make an awful fuss when I go up there. If I go up to Glyncorrwg, I'm not home here until about four o'clock in the morning. Men going to the Abbey bring me home, you know, we have a late drinking session.

In fact, Tom felt that his father's knowledge of his career and his sexuality was a positive development because he was, in general, 'very broadminded, everybody loved him for his broadminded-ness'. By implication, this was also true of the wider community. Tom's interest in dressing up in women's clothes had begun early: 'I was awfully interested in ladies clothes, and always dress-ing up as a woman, before I left school really. So now, and if my sisters had anything new, a hat, a coat, or a dress ... I wasn't happy until I tried it on.' Many of his childhood friends were girls and he 'never played football or cricket or anything', preferring instead to join in with hopscotch and skipping on the pavement outside his house. Through these experiences, Tom picked up the mannerisms and comportments that he was later to use to great effect and to popular delight as a drag artist.

Tom Davies was not the only Welsh female impersonator in the early part of the twentieth century, although he was the only one whose memories were recorded and whose sexuality can be offered with any degree of certainty. The others, such as Percy Meye (or Maye, as it was sometimes written), Will Thomas, Louis van Della or Tom Barger, whose careers took them all over Wales between the mid-1890s and the end of the First World War, are much more secretive. Several of them married and regarded impersonation not as a transgressive act, necessarily, but as part of a legitimate career in the music hall and theatre. Some were feted as the favourite performers of the towns in which they most regularly performed, as Louis van Della was in Aberdare,[4] although he had competition from Lawrence Lisle, an impersonator of burlesque routines.[5] In the north, the most popular artist was Tom Barger, who promised audiences 'hilarity without vulgarity'.[6]

Percy Meye had perhaps the highest profile of all and first came to notice performing at the opening ceremony of Aberystwyth pier in the summer of 1896. His 'skirt dances' were said to have caused 'much amusement' and he quickly established himself as an in-demand performer. He returned regularly as part of Henry Collins's Minstrel Troupe until the turn of the new century when he moved to Rhyl and eventually to the Rhondda, where he found work in picture palaces and theatres. At the Tivoli in Pentre, Meye was introduced to audiences as 'unique', 'realistic' and able to impersonate 'the lady artistes with perfect ease'.[7] As the *Rhondda Leader* noted, 'one who frequents the Tivoli thinks that Percy "Meye" be a lady for the following reasons. He sings fine "airs", sports false "hair", and seems fonder of the trousers than the skirt.'[8] As an artist of growing stature, Meye appeared in theatres all over Britain in the early 1900s. In London, he was feted as 'really startling in [his] realism', in Bristol as one of the best impersonators to appear on stage in the city, and in Hartlepool as wearing 'make-up [which] defies identity'.[9] An essential part of Percy Meye's act was his replication of the female voice both for singing and delivery of comedic turns. According to one industry journal, he had a 'good falsetto' which enhanced the perceived realism.[10]

It was easy to go to the theatre to watch a man dressed up as a woman performing on stage. It was regarded by Victorian and Edwardian audiences as entirely normal (as it had been for centuries). On the reverse, it was just as easy to sit in the same seats and watch women dressing up as men. Nationally famous male impersonators such as Vesta Tilley, Phyllis Broughton, Hetty King or Lillian Bishop travelled frequently to theatres in Wales where they were warmly welcomed, and there were local artists who mimicked their acts to more modest acclaim. When Vesta Tilley appeared at the Cardiff Empire in 1907, the venue was reportedly packed out by her many local fans.[11] A decade earlier, to accompany an interview with the *South Wales Echo*, she was sketched in male attire complete with jacket and trousers, boater hat, and waistcoat.[12] It was a remarkable presentation given the radical and political nature of women 'donning male attire' – suffrage campaigners wore men's clothing to protest against their lack of voting rights – but it was consistent with the emerging idea of the New Woman who fought for rights and sexual and social freedoms and for greater recognition of the gender iniquities of turn-of-the-century Britain.[13] As Phyllis Broughton explained to one Aberystwyth journalist, 'I made a raid on my brother's wardrobe, and for a fortnight, at home, I absolutely lived in a suit of his clothes in order to get thoroughly used to it.'[14]

Outside the theatre or music hall, for women to wear men's clothing, especially trousers, was a striking act of defiance – sticking two fingers up to the authorities. Janet Pugh of Llangwm near Corwen, a prominent figure in the tithe wars of the 1890s, often adopted 'a bowler hat and cord trousers'.[15] Politics was not on the mind of Maria Evans when she appeared, heavily pregnant, before magistrates in Cardiff in 1856 charged with disorderly conduct in Bute Street. She did so 'in male attire' and claimed that she 'only intended to have a bit of fun'. The magistrates were not amused and sent her to the workhouse.[16] In court women wearing trousers was code for prostitution: 'a woman might have been seen walking down Thompson Street, Barry Dock, last Thursday evening,' remarked the *Barry Dock News* indicatively in 1892, 'clothed in male attire.'[17] The *Evening Express* sniped in similar terms a few years later about Ellen O'Neil. She was 'a very advanced type of the New Woman. On Wednesday she appeared in the dock at Penarth Police Court fully accoutred in male attire.'[18]

In the decades before the moral panic around Radclyffe Hall's 1928 novel, *The Well of Loneliness*, with its appeals to the naturalness of lesbian love and for 'the right to our existence', phrases such as 'in male attire' or 'close companion' could sometimes be read, by those in the know, as indications of same-sex attraction. But not always, and iterations need to be read with caution. Notions of clothing as an 'encoded "uniform"' evolved slowly, and 'readings (whether of clothing, visual images, or stories about women living with other women in "Close companionship") varied accordingly among those who knew, those who knew nothing, and those who wished they didn't know.'[19] It is problematic to assume that all women observed or arrested in male clothes were sexually transgressive, since the act meant various things to different individuals, but at the same time it is no less problematic to assume that there were no lesbians before the twentieth century even though the term did not gain popular currency until the 1930s. In the absence of a public culture of lesbianism, same-sex desire amongst women often passed by unnoticed and unremarked upon and cross-dressing frowned upon. 'Where the fun lies', blustered one Cardiff newspaper in

1869, 'only the idiots who indulge in the practice would be able to explain. Perhaps the knowledge that the pastime is not unattended with risk may give it a zest which the casual observer would fail to appreciate.'[20]

The contrast to this complex world of cross-dressing, in which Tom Davies and others revelled and found sustainable employment, lay in the tortured self-marginalisation of men such as the novelist and short story writer Rhys Davies.[21] For him, the coalfield was an impossible environment in which to live as a homosexual, and led to depression and isolation. The Valleys were possessed of a form of masculinity that the writer was unable to adjust to, and in later years he described the coalfield as a gaol from which he could not escape however much he tried. He would eventually find peace in London, a city which provided him with 'a rainbow wash of the mind'.[22] These themes underpinned his writing, although he went to great lengths to disguise the truth of his inner self: even his name was altered, he was born Vivian Rees Davies.

The experiences of Tom Davies and Rhys Davies, their separate reactions to their own sexuality and the social and cultural context into which they were born and grew up, serve as a reminder that personal experience of same-sex desire in the early twentieth century varied and was never uniformly negative. The southern coalfield, especially, was neither uniquely repressive, as most biographers and scholars of Rhys Davies have assumed, nor was it completely tolerant as Tom Davies's experiences might suggest. The boundaries of sexuality and gender lay somewhere in between – hence the discrete responses to that world of heavy industry and masculine strength. Although much changed legally and culturally over the course of their lives, the division which their experiences serve to illustrate remained apparent:

there were those who found acceptance, perhaps by means of a certain type of work, and those who felt uncomfortable, even oppressed, and left. Tom and Rhys Davies were indicative of a part of Welsh society which was mostly hidden from view but nevertheless in plain sight.

For centuries, the boundaries of close friendship, intimacy and same-sex desire were carefully traversed by men and women, and there was a boundary between acceptable intimacy between two friends or companions of the same gender and 'the forbidden intimacy of homosexuality'.[23] This was a society in which privacy was limited, the sharing of beds common, and ideas of kinship and family more flexible than modern nuclear bonds. To be an individual's bedfellow or bedmate, *cywely* or *erchwyniog* as it was in Welsh, was not limited to a spouse but someone for whom affect, intimacy and patronage were apparent or desired characteristics. Likewise, if sexual activity before the eighteenth century was 'characterised by mutual masturbation, much kissing and fondling, and long hours spent in mutual touching', then the boundary between transgressive and non-transgressive behaviour was probably quite different from twenty-first-century acceptability, with an emphasis on penetrative sex as the basis of impropriety.[24] Kissing, a common greeting in the early modern period, was governed by the difference between 'a civil and honest manner to express our love to one another' or a 'civil courtesy' and the more transgressive embrace used 'in wanton dalliance between those who are light and lascivious'.[25]

In other words, a whole range of characteristics indicative of friendship and emotional intimacy could be misconceived as innocent rather than based on same-sex desire, or ignored until the boundary of physicality was crossed. Indeed, masturbation and sodomy, which were sometimes bound together under the latter term, attracted attention not only because they were considered grave sins but also because they were physical acts and forms of 'pollution'. Ostensibly, sodomy was the preserve of ecclesiastical courts before the introduction of a secular legal framework which criminalised the 'detestable and abominable vice of buggery committed with mankind or beast' during the reign of Henry VIII. First passed in England in 1533, in the context of the suppression of the monasteries, the legislation was extended to Wales in 1542 as part of the Acts of Union. It was then repealed in 1547, reinstated by Edward VI, and repealed again in 1553 by Mary I, who regarded all sexual crime as the province of the Church. The law was eventually reinstated by Elizabeth in 1563. Yet neither in England nor Wales was sodomy a major theme. In London, just one example has been found amongst more than 20,000 cases heard at the city's ecclesiastical courts between 1470 and 1516. The case, which arose because the defendant was heard boasting of his sexual activity, was dropped before any verdict was reached.[26]

Nor was London any different from other parts of England or Wales, and in Scotland sodomy seems not to have been prosecuted at all.[27] Absence of prosecution was unlikely to have meant that same-sex desire was completely absent from society, of course, or even that early modern society lacked any notion of 'homosexual' behaviour, but the silence of the legal record nevertheless gives pause for thought. What exactly was the boundary between same-sex desire expressed through companionship and accepted activities such as bed sharing, kissing and petting, and the physical forms of desire likely to give rise to gossip or a court case? And if sodomy was as grave a sin – or criminal misdemeanour (which conveyed a range of other meanings from masturbation to suspected Catholicism and treason) – as the law suggested, how was it policed if not by the ecclesiastical or secular courts? Did this also mean that they were 'deeply repressed' and 'below the documentary radar'?[28] 'On the basis of modern ideas', suggests historian Martin Ingram, '[it] might be expected that homosexual practices would feature prominently in legal records.' Their absence suggests that 'the pursuit of same-sex relationships was effectively not part of the normal pattern of legal regulation'.[29]

The archival 'gap' is both frustrating and compelling, certainly in comparison with those parts of Europe, such as Florence, Bruges, and Spain, where prosecution rates were considerable and documentary evidence much more complex and readily available. It also helps to explain the relative lack of interest shown by historians of late medieval and early modern Wales in same-sex desire.[30] The difficulties involved in discussing or analysing the nature and experience of same-sex desire, let alone 'homosexuality', before the eighteenth century, certainly amongst ordinary people, are numerous and involve a good deal of supposition and inference. And yet it is not impossible, given the persistence of 'noise and rhetorical dirt'.[31] Wales, in this period, was a largely, though not exclusively, monoglot Welsh-speaking society, so care must be taken in drawing too great an inference from linguistic and written evidence apparent in English. In Welsh there was much less rhetorical 'noise'. Whereas crimes such as adultery, fornication, sexual incontinence and prostitution, which were already significantly present in ecclesiastical court records, had a rich and expanding vocabulary, the equivalent for sodomy was limited. The oldest terms appear to have entered the language in the Elizabethan period, providing translations for the legal framework introduced by the Buggery Act on the one hand, or for biblical narratives on the other.

William Salesbury's 1567 translation of the New Testament referred both to the act, *bwggeryddion*, and the actor, *gwrw-gydwyr*, to render into Welsh that passage of Paul's first epistle to Timothy which William Tyndale had translated into English as 'them that defile themselves with mankynde'. Neither had appeared in Salesbury's dictionary published in 1547, however, so were probably of relatively recent invention. William Morgan's translation published in 1588 provided a third term, *sodomiaidd*. In the early eighteenth century, a fourth term, *anlladrwydd gyda bechgyn*, indecency with men, appeared. Bestiality, *llwdngar*, which was considered as unnatural as sodomy and linked in legal terms, was apparent much earlier, although in the eighteenth century this evolved into *anifeiligrwydd*, literally meaning copulation between man and animal, as part of a general linguistic separation between bestial relations and same-sex desire. The language used to describe buggery and buggers, then, at least in terms of the evidence from surviving texts, was formulaic and focused on the sexual act as set out in law. So much for the assistance, and persistence, of whispers in a world otherwise seemingly silent.

But given that much of the language used to describe sex was allusory – masturbation was known as 'self-pollution' (or *hunan-halogedigaeth* in seventeenth-century Welsh) – placing too much stress on the limitations of direct translations is to misinterpret a rich culture full of inference and word play. What else to make of Dafydd ap Gwilym's 'sceptre that causes lust' or his 'trouser problem personified'? Or, indeed, Gwerful Mechain's celebration of the vagina, female sexuality and the arousing allure of the female body? Whereas historians and critics of the early twentieth century could scoff that 'Gwerful Mechain is nothing more than a whore but in her own century singing dirty songs was more or less a common thing to do, especially on the continent', we can now recognise a different spirit and can be sensitive to the genuine purpose of her artistic expression.[32] Sexual expression, including of same-sex desire, was by no means unusual, nor was there a resolute separation of the religious and the erotic: the two existed side by side.[33]

The rich playfulness of late medieval poetry was steadily submerged: first by a poor, conservative society and then by a Nonconformist cultural ethos committed to temperance and sexual abstinence. Few in Wales talked about same-sex desire. Not that there appeared to be any great need, since buggery remained stubbornly absent from the courts. Although the early modern period was a 'golden age' of litigation, and cases of adultery, fornication, bastardy and clandestine marriage, were common, the courts rarely heard cases involving accusations of same-sex desire.[34] Likewise the surviving records of the Courts of Great Session, the highest criminal court in most of Wales from the 1540s to 1830, suggests that judges were little troubled. Between 1730 and 1830, just twenty four cases of sodomy and buggery were heard, a tiny fraction of the more than twenty thousand cases presented during that century. Even considering that sexual offences were a minor part of the court's business – around 200 cases in that period, mostly relating to the rape or attempted rape of women – this was a very small number. There were fifty eight indictments in Bristol alone between 1730 and 1800.[35]

Despite such paucity there were clear patterns. Counties with relatively large centres of population presented more cases than did rural counties. For the entire period between 1730 and 1830 there were no indictments for sodomy from Anglesey, Cardiganshire, Caernarfonshire, Carmarthenshire, Meirionnydd, or Montgomeryshire. Denbighshire and Radnorshire had a small number between them. Those accused of sodomy, or the attempt, were generally not members of elite society but ordinary individuals living in towns and working as bakers, shoemakers or hatters, or they were sailors or clergymen. Those making the accusations occupied a similar stratum of society. Only one case seems to have been successfully prosecuted: the accused, David Thomas, a yeoman from Haverfordwest and a member of the Pembroke county militia, was fined by the court after being found guilty of sodomy. All other cases were either dismissed as having no true bill or the accused was found not guilty by the jury. The death penalty, which was the ultimate punishment for anyone found guilty of sodomy, was never applied.

Following the abolition of the Great Sessions in 1830, and the uniform application of the Assize system across Wales, the number of sodomy cases per decade rose steadily in absolute terms from about half a dozen in the 1830s to nearly fifty by the 1870s, before declining in subsequent decades. In rural counties indictments continued to be rare – just one in Cardiganshire from the mid-1830s to the mid-1890s – and fewer than half a dozen in Anglesey, Caernarfonshire, Carmarthenshire, Meirionnydd, and Radnorshire. Pembrokeshire and the industrial counties of the north-east, Denbighshire and Flintshire, provided a second tier of indictments – numerous in comparison with rural counties but noticeably fewer than those of Glamorgan and Monmouthshire which together were responsible for more than half of all proceedings for same-sex offences. This trend was also true of sexual attacks on women across the nineteenth century, although in rural areas a good deal of indecent behaviour was reported to the police (and duly logged in daily occurrence books) but was not subsequently prosecuted in the sessions courts of the Assizes. 'There was', wrote David Jones in his study of nineteenth-century crime, 'an unspoken feeling in many sections of society that such matters were best kept out of court.'[36] This seems also to have been true of same-sex desire.

Such beliefs survived the attempt in the mid-1880s to revive public morals and to make it easier to prosecute men for sexual activity with other men. The Labouchère Amendment to the 1885 Criminal Law Amendment Act, named for its proposer, Liberal MP Henry Labouchère, was justified on the basis that the existing law on sodomy was 'insufficient to deal with it, because the offence had to be proved by an accessory, and many other offences very much of the same nature were not regarded as crimes at all'. In proposing the introduction of the crime of gross indecency, Labouchère insisted that 'parliament armed the guardians of public morality with full powers to deal with this offence'.[37] The consequence was an extension of the legal powers of the police and the courts but to apparently little effect. Ten years after the amendment was passed, the annual rate of prosecution for same-sex offences in Wales was between half a dozen and a dozen, much as it had been prior to the change in the law.

For all this legal absence, the public was not naïve. It understood what *might* occur should two men sneak off to the latrine together, as John Nash and Henry Jones discovered in October 1887 when they were arrested on a charge of committing gross indecency in a lavatory at Maindy Barracks in Cardiff. Nash was thirty four and a corporal, Jones a twenty-year-old private. When the case came before the Assizes the following month, the two men explained that their intentions had been misinterpreted and that they had not, in fact, gone to the latrine 'for a wrongful purpose'. In any case, they argued, 'it was improbable they should have acted as described'. Despite claims that their defence testimony was merely a 'rambling statement', the pair were acquitted by the jury and discharged.[38] The public also no longer relied on allusion and inference to suggest character traits in men. In the south, they spoke of the *sioni fenyw*; in the north they discussed the *cadi ffan*. English-speakers referred to the effeminate man. Like Tom Davies these men may have been interested in women's clothes and dancing and performing on the stage, whether in drag or not, but certainly by the end of the nineteenth century they were no longer hidden from view.

Notes

1. South Wales Miners' Library, AUD/328: Interview with Tom Davies conducted by Merfyn Jones, 1 December 1973.
2. Roger Baker, *Drag: A History of Female Impersonation in the Performing Arts* (New York, 1995), pp. 191–2.
3. Compare the experience of John Rowlands, who insisted on going to school in what was then regarded as 'girl's attire'. He eventually turned up wearing culottes. *EEx*, 11 March 1897.
4. *Aberdare Leader*, 24 January 1903.
5. *Merthyr Times*, 14 February 1895.
6. *Rhyl Journal*, 16 August 1902.
7. *Rhondda Leader*, 22 June 1907, 11 December 1909.
8. *Rhondda Leader*, 26 December 1908.
9. *The Era*, 26 October 1901; *The Bristol Magpie*, 20 September 1906; *Hartlepool Northern Daily Mail*, 16 May 1899.
10. *Music Hall and Theatre Review*, 5 December 1902.
11. *EEx*, 16 April 1907.
12. *SWE*, 23 June 1897.
13. Sally Ledger, *The New Woman: Fiction and Feminism at the Fin de Siècle* (Manchester, 1997).
14. *The Aberystwyth Observer*, 16 November 1893.
15. *Llangollen Advertiser*, 8 December 1916.
16. *Cardiff and Merthyr Guardian*, 8 November 1856.
17. *Barry Dock News*, 4 November 1892.
18. *EEx*, 2 January 1896.
19. Laura Doan, *Fashioning Sapphism: The Origins of a Modern English Lesbian Culture* (New York, 2001), p. xiv.

20. *Cardiff and Merthyr Guardian*, 24 April 1869.

21. Huw Osborne, *Rhys Davies* (Cardiff, 2009); Meic Stephens, *Rhys Davies: A Writer's Life* (Cardigan, 2013).

22. Rhys Davies, *A Print of the Hare's Foot* (Bridgend, 1997 edn), p. 109.

23. Alan Bray, 'Homosexuality and the Signs of Male Friendship in Elizabethan England', *History Workshop*, 29 (1990), 3.

24. Tim Hitchcock, 'The Reformulation of Sexual Knowledge in Eighteenth-century England', *Signs: Journal of Women in Culture and Society*, 37/4 (2012). Although Angela Muir has recently argued that the changes apparent in England were probably more modest in Wales owing to the absence of equivalently translated sexual advice literature. Angela Joy Muir, 'Courtship, Sex and Poverty: Illegitimacy in Eighteenth-Century Wales', *Social History*, 43/1 (2018), 56–80.

25. John Downame, *Foure treatises, tending to disswade all Christians from foure no lesse heinous then common sinnes* (1609), p. 201. Cited in Martin Ingram, 'Sexual manners: the other face of civility in early modern England', in Peter Burke, Brian Harrison and Paul Slack (eds), *Civil Histories: Essays Presented to Sir Keith Thomas* (Oxford, 2000), p. 96.

26. R. B. Outhwaite, *The Rise and Fall of the English Ecclesiastical Courts, 1500–1860* (Cambridge), p. 59.

27. R. H. Helmholz, *The Canon Law and Ecclesiastical Jurisdiction from 597 to the 1640s* (Oxford), p. 629; P. G. Maxwell-Stuart's chapter, '"Wild, filthie, execrabill, detestabill, and unnatural sin": bestiality in early modern Scotland', in Tom Betteridge (ed.), *Sodomy in Early Modern Europe* (Manchester, 2002).

28. Shannon McSheffrey, *Marriage, Sex, and Civic Culture in Medieval London* (Philadelphia, 2006), p. 149.

29. Martin Ingram, *Carnal Knowledge: Regulating Sex in England, 1470–1600* (Cambridge, 2017), pp. 34–8.

30. Although several rich studies of homosexuality in early modern England have been written including Alan Bray, *Homosexuality in Renaissance England* (London, 1982) and Bruce R. Smith, *Homosexual Desire in Shakespeare's England: A Cultural Poetics* (Chicago, 1991). Laura Gowing, Michael Hunter and Miri Rubin (eds), *Love, Friendship and Faith in Europe, 1300–1800* (London, 2006) and Betteridge (ed.), *Sodomy*, provide comparative surveys of the period.

31. Tom Linkinen, *Same-sex Sexuality in Late Medieval English Culture* (Amsterdam, 2015), p. 10.

32. Leslie Harries, *Barddoniaeth Huw Cae Llwyd, Ieuan ap Huw Cae Llwyd, Ieuan Dyfi, a Gwerful Mechain* (Unpublished MA Thesis, Swansea, 1933), 26.

33. I have been guided here by Katie Gramich's observations on Gwerful Mechain. Katie Gramich (ed.), *The Works of Gwerful Mechain* (London, 2018). See also, Dafydd Johnston (ed.), *Medieval Welsh Erotic Poetry* (Bridgend, 1998).

34. Richard Suggett, 'Slander in Early Modern Wales', *Bulletin of the Board of Celtic Studies*, 39 (1992), 149.

35. Steve Poole, '"Bringing great shame upon this city": Sodomy, the Courts, and the Civic Idiom in Eighteenth-century Bristol', *Urban History*, 34/1 (2007), 119.

36. David J. V. Jones, *Crime in Nineteenth-century Wales* (Cardiff, 1992), p. 80.

37. Henry Labouchère, cited in Harry Cocks, *Nameless Offences: Homosexual Desire in the Nineteenth Century* (London, 2009), p. 17.

38. *SWE*, 19 October, 9 November 1887; *CT*, 12 November 1887; *WM*, 10 November 1887.

CHAPTER TWO

Legal Limitations

Fred was born in Cadoxton in August 1894, the youngest in a family of eleven children.[1] His father was a stonemason and an alcoholic; his mother, a dressmaker, died when Fred was just thirteen. In 1908 he left school and went to work as a labourer before moving on to his brother-in-law's plastering firm. By the time he was sixteen, Fred was working as a hod carrier at Ranks Mill in Barry Dock. At the outbreak of war in 1914, he joined the army although he was initially rejected on medical grounds. It was in the army that Fred was first able to explore the impulses which he had had since childhood and to associate his own feelings with ideas about 'shagging' which were typical of conversation amongst the boys of Cadoxton and Barry. It was with his friend Geoff that he had sex for the first time. Fred takes up the story,

It had never entered my mind before. I was always scared. But we used to put our arms around one another and nothing happened for weeks and weeks till this particular day. We'd had our bath and were sunbathing and Geoff got a hard on and he rolled over on top of me, and he started making love

like that. Of course that's when it all started. And oh it was
lovely. I'll never forget it. Never forget it.

A few years later, shortly after returning home to Barry, and
entirely by chance, Fred met another young man with whom he
had an affair – an eighteen-year-old farm hand. Fred's honesty
illustrates that, despite anxiety and the probability that expo-
sure could have life-changing implications, the men who were
arrested and prosecuted for gross indecency found themselves
in such positions because they had chosen to have sex with
other men.[2] It is unlikely that those men considered themselves
'homosexuals' or shared an identity, which in London was 'rooted
in the law and defiance of the law'.[3] As Fred explained, 'I didn't
hear the word "homosexual" till I came out of the army.' But who
were these men who had sex with or desired other men? What
sort of work did they do? Where did they come from?

The cohort of men arrested and prosecuted for gross indecency, buggery and the attempts, at least before the Second World
War included soldiers, sailors, tailors, hairdressers, labourers,
firemen, hawkers, colliers, chimney sweeps, bakers, riggers,
cooks, railwaymen, painters and the unemployed. Just a handful,
in Glamorgan and Monmouthshire at least, were students, musi-
cians, actors, clerks and school teachers. In a society enlarged by
high levels of immigration and characterised by a high degree
of labour mobility, the cohort also reflected racial and cultural
diversity. In other words, these men represented a complete
cross-section of working-class society: the purpose of this chapter is to provide a collective biography of some of them and to
examine the ways in which same-sex desire was expressed and
policed at the local level. Inevitably this is a story focused on a
small number of locations, almost entirely along the coastline

of Glamorgan and Monmouthshire. But there are exceptions. Between 1908 and 1915, for instance, there were only three trials in Merthyr Tydfil involving men who had sex with other men; in the 1920s fewer than a handful of men were arrested; and none at all in the borough between 1930 and 1942.[4]

Although the figures were higher in Cardiff than in Merthyr Tydfil, they were nevertheless modest in comparison to other cities in Britain. Between 1921 and 1936, approximately fifty men were subject to criminal proceedings for same-sex activity – an average of three a year. The rate was similar in Swansea. Those arrested were unfortunate to have been caught: the police were not active in pursuing same-sex offences and did not seek to entrap men who had sex with other men, as the Metropolitan Police did in parts of London. Yet there is also no doubt that the police engaged in profiling those whom they considered to be 'homosexuals' or possessed of homosexual 'traits'. This procedure drew on characteristics identified by the Metropolitan Police in their observations of the queer subcultures in London, and was transmitted to county constabularies and city and borough forces through the *Police Gazette*. This was an internal newsletter published by the Metropolitan Police designed to assist in the arrest of absconded or multiple offenders.

The entry for Alfred Wilson, a twenty year-old from Leicester, which was published in the *Police Gazette* in May 1918, was typical. Five feet four and a half inches tall with a fresh complex, brown hair and grey eyes, he was said to dress respectably and was fairly well spoken but he wore his hair long and was 'believed to be a confirmed sodomite'.[5] Phrases such as 'effeminate voice', 'powders and paints his face' or 'in female attire', particularly in conjunction with previous convictions for gross indecency, were sufficient for the police to make assumptions about a person's sexual inclinations.[6] Thus in 1916, Cardiff police arrested Tom Allen, a sailor from San Francisco, on a charge of burglary but willingly drew attention to his previous convictions for gross indecency.[7] Association with music hall entertainment provided a similar pathology. Nor was such profiling entirely limited to men. Women whose voices were 'masculine', who had a 'masculine appearance', or were seen 'in male attire' were similarly subject to police presumption. This became more sophisticated in the 1930s with the development of more clearly defined lesbian identities.

Use of profiling continued throughout the twentieth century albeit with modernised language. In 1962, Newport Borough Police issued a notice appealing for a chef who had absconded from the town on charges of fraud – he had tendered a worthless cheque to a shopkeeper. He was depicted as having thinning, brown hair, hazel eyes and an effeminate voice – he was a 'homosexual'.[8] Another case, this time from Pembrokeshire, involved a man wanted for larceny. He was described as having dark brown wavy hair and blue eyes, he sometimes wore spectacles and was often seen in clerical grey or green tweed. He had 'homosexual tendencies'.[9] The widespread use of these character traits by the middle part of the twentieth century suggests that a formalised homosexual 'identity' was by then part of the consciousness of the state and we can be sure that if police officers made assumptions, so did everyone else.[10] But it was not always this way.

In July 1898, Daniel John Drew Codner failed to appear at the Pembrokeshire Assizes to answer charges of gross indecency with James Jones in Pembroke earlier in the year; his name was published in the *Police Gazette* together with a description.[11] Born in Woking in 1852, Codner was a church organist and composer, and had previously worked at St Bride's Church, Fleet Street, Christ Church in Bromley, and between 1894 and 1896 was the organist at St David's Cathedral.[12] Although he retired because of eye strain and back pain, he remained in Pembrokeshire until his arrest in April 1898.[13] Perhaps fearful of the personal trauma that a court case (and associated gossip) would bring, Codner fled the county leaving the men who had provided his bail, notably the Rev. W. G. Spurrell, canon of St David's, to explain his absence.[14] Despite a warrant being issued for his arrest, Codner evaded the Pembrokeshire authorities and resumed his music career in the south-east of England: he found work playing at a church in Hastings and regularly performed in London and East Anglia. He even sought marriage, although there is no evidence that the proposed ceremony ever took place.

In the autumn of 1901, whilst at the church of St Peter Mancroft in Norwich, Codner met George Parker. In early December, Codner was arrested again, this time on a charge of buggery, and sentenced to ten years' penal servitude at the county Assizes. During the court proceedings, Codner pleaded that he had 'been drinking at Ely and had a longer bout than usual, and that when he came to Norwich his head gave way'. He also explained that he had been 'subject to mental aberration all his life' (described in other accounts as 'inherited insanity'[15]), a defence which relied on the excruciating testimony of his mother, Elizabeth, who described the mental collapse of her husband and her son's similar descent into 'madness'.[16] Codner spent five years at Dartmoor Prison before being released on licence in January 1907. The cumulative effects of alcoholism, prison and the stress of the trial were substantial, and on his release Codner moved in with his mother. He died of sudden heart failure in November 1913, aged sixty two.[17] His otherwise successful career in music had been ruined by two sexual encounters at opposite ends of the country and a lifetime's abuse of alcohol to douse his own desire.

José Escamilla was a sailor. Born in Spain in 1886, he was thirty-two years old at the time of his arrest in Swansea shortly after New Year, 1918, on charges of gross indecency. Five feet six with black hair, he was regarded by the press as typically Iberian. He was sentenced to fifteen months' hard labour at the assizes, although his partner, George Pirie, faced no charges. Shortly before his release, in the spring of 1919, Escamilla fell ill and was transferred to Swansea General Hospital. His subsequent death was recorded as due to exhaustion and tuberculosis.[18] We can speculate, given the date, that Escamilla may well have died because of the contemporary influenza epidemic typically known as Spanish Flu.[19] A month before Escamilla's death, every school in Swansea had been ordered shut and children were banned from cinemas to prevent the spread of disease which had claimed the lives of more than eighty people, while related pneumonia had killed more than sixty.[20] Unfortunately little else is known about José Escamilla, and his trial at the Glamorgan Assizes in 1918 was not reported to the same extent as Daniel Codner's had been.

The same year that Escamilla was arrested and imprisoned in Swansea, Abdulla Taslameden was arrested and charged with sexual offences in Cardiff.[21] He was twenty-two, a fireman from the Middle East working in the merchant navy and based in Cardiff only for a brief moment. The encounter with George Halloran that summer resulted in a twelve-month prison sentence. His police photograph shows a young man, well dressed in winged collar and tie, with dark curly hair and a small moustache. It was his first known offence in the city, and his last.

Osgar Ali was different. He also worked on board merchant ships as a cook. Born in Mumbai, India, he had initially travelled to Britain under a different name, Basil Mahomed, but adopted his new identity after being arrested and convicted of petty larceny in Liverpool.[22] In the summer of 1916, his ship landed in Barry. During the turn-around period, he met a local man, John Wilson, and the pair had sex. They soon found themselves at the police court charged with buggery. Ali was subsequently sentenced to six months' hard labour at the Assizes, although John Wilson was not charged with any crime. It was similar for Ahmed Said, a fireman, who landed at Penarth dock that year, met a local man called James Swanson, and was then imprisoned for committing buggery. Swanson faced no charges.

There are certainly grounds for assuming that in many such instances the court looked more favourably on the local 'victim' compared with a 'foreign perpetrator', and in several cases the latter was removed from Britain altogether. Louis Perlin, a Jewish immigrant from Eastern Europe, was living in Cardiff and working as a tailor at the time of his arrest in January 1910. He was twenty-one. Charged with gross indecency with a local man, Daniel Sullivan, at a house in Havelock Street in Temperance Town, Perlin appeared at the Spring Assizes and was ultimately acquitted.[23] However, and despite his innocence, the judge recommended Perlin for deportation; Sullivan faced no charges whatsoever. Although Perlin was not immediately deported, he understood that Britain was unlikely to be a comfortable place for him to live in, and in 1912 he boarded a passenger liner bound for Newfoundland. Unable to settle there, he returned to Britain before trying his luck in the United States in December 1915. He was refused entry upon arrival in New York City and deported back to Britain. From that moment, he disappeared from the record, his life had been thrown into disarray even though he was innocent of the charges brought against him.

Demetrios Delonghu, on the other hand, was charged with and sentenced to nearly a year in prison for committing buggery with William Henry Baldwin. Delonghu was born in Mytilene on the island of Lesbos in March 1887 and arrived in Cardiff in the summer of 1934. His dark hair steadily turning grey and a distinctive cross on his right forearm, Delonghu was older than the sailors normally arrested for same-sex offences in Cardiff in the inter-war years but his position on board ship – fireman – was entirely typical. On handing down sentence, the judge insisted that Delonghu be served with a deportation order once it was completed, and on release from Cardiff prison in April 1935 he was handed to the city police and made to leave the country. In many respects, Delonghu was more fortunate in his treatment than the teenager with whom he had had sex. Baldwin was detained indefinitely at Ely hospital on psychiatric grounds. John Gevas had similar treatment following his arrest and imprisonment in 1912 for having sex with fifteen-year-old William Cook. Cook received a four week custodial sentence in part because he had a previous conviction for stealing a pair of boots. Gevas, on the other hand, was imprisoned for a year and then deported back to his native Greece.

It was quite likely that each of these men returned to the merchant marine after their release from prison or their deportation. This is what happened to Andros Kokolas. Born in Kefalonia, Greece, in 1891, he went to sea in October 1918 as a steward. His ship landed in Barry in February 1919. Whilst staying in the town he met Charles Shord and soon afterwards found himself in front of magistrates charged with buggery. The judge at the Assizes sentenced him to six months' hard labour, and on release he returned to the merchant marine as a fireman. It was also what happened to Francis Darmanin, a fireman from Birgu, Malta, who was arrested in 1921 for a liaison with William George Brignall, a teenage labourer from Treherbert. At the time of his arrest, Darmanin was not quite thirty although the police thought he was closer to forty, given his appearance. His police photograph showed a worn face, thinning greying hair, and a thick moustache, which was in stark contrast with his merchant navy registration card which showed a vibrant and youthful face, thick, dark brown hair, and a quirky smile. The change clearly confused the police. Darmanin received a sentence of eighteen months, which he spent in Cardiff prison before returning to sea. Brignall was bound over to keep the peace and slipped out of the record until his premature death in 1932. He was just twenty-seven.

Encounters such as these might well have fashioned in the public consciousness particular notions of the sailor, or at the very least reinforced them. As Laura Tabili has observed, 'crews of certain lines were alleged havens for homosexual and transvestites.' But this seems not to have been the case. Indeed, these arrests and the accompanying trials prompted very little public debate either about the existence (even persistence) of same-sex offences in ports or about 'deviant foreign practices', a theme very much in evidence in the policing and presentation of prostitution. The nearest that same-sex desire came to being portrayed as a 'foreign' practice was an article published in a Swansea newspaper in 1919. It described night-time activities on Quay Parade, the heart of the docklands area of the town and a short walk from Wind Street.

> Last night the writer, in just passing through this hundred
> yards or so saw: a) a man evidently in drink vomiting over

the pavement; b) three foreigners collected around a girl of
15, whom one of them was affectionately hugging; two men
(foreigners) in dungarees committing an offence against
elementary decency in an archway where there happened to
be just sufficient lamplight to enable passers-by to see what
they were up to. Other groups of foreigners were collected,
some in drink, arguing, with a heat and in a tone that suggested a likely quarrel.

He continued:

This mixed crowd loafs about usually until eleven o'clock
at night, sometimes longer, for portions of it take refuge in
places neighbouring where it cannot be touched, with occasional scenes of solicitation, the open consorting of men
with bad characters, acts of gross indecency, drunkenness,
brawling, the association of young girls with foreigners of
continental habits and notions of morality – some, and sometimes almost all, of these offences may be witnessed every
night, under the arches or in dark doorways.[24]

Such material was intended to scandalise, but it had little
impact and prompted no public debate about the morality of
same-sex desire. Few people in Swansea cared. And yet they
did care about prostitution, as they did in Cardiff. There was
an active attempt by the police and the media in both places
to frame the persistence of prostitution as a foreign practice using language replete with contemporary ideas about
race. The 'white' population of Cardiff, especially, was being
drawn into networks of sexual degeneracy by Greek and Maltese
pimps who then sold the services of 'British' prostitutes to

'foreign' sailors. There was similar invective against mixed marriages.

A key figure in the policing of these aspects of inter-war Cardiff was the city's chief constable James Arthur Wilson.[25] His views on the racialised nature of prostitution are well known. He believed that the cafés of Bute Street had replaced brothels and rough pubs because they could operate under the guise of quasi-legitimacy with 'waitresses and dance partners cater[ing] for the sexual licence of the floating population', and that sailors who frequented them were in 'intimate contact with the female sex of the white race, principally those ... who are prostitutes or women of loose moral character'. He was also on record describing Cardiff as a 'sober and well-conducted city and port' despite the 'vicious habits of a section of the floating population'.[26] Yet he did not draw the same kind of links between sailors and same-sex activity despite the relative regularity of cases in the city's police courts, and thus pointed to a relative tolerance of certain forms of behaviour: 'The public do not understand how far the police can go in suppressing the behaviour of amorous couples. Amorous behaviour, however distasteful to conventional people, is no offence against the law.'[27] The contrast with his views on prostitution and the vigour with which it was policed was striking, but Wilson had previously been the Chief Constable of the Merthyr Tydfil Borough Police where there had been little real attempt either to pursue men who had, or attempted to have, sex with other men – in contrast to Wilson's strident attempts to eradicate prostitution in the town. His successor in Merthyr, David Morgan Davies, seems to have been similarly focused. But why?

Such a stance was not limited to the police forces of Wales, of course, and therein lies at least part of the answer: this was the normal approach to policing outside London and cities such as Liverpool. In much of the north of England, limited police resources meant that pursuing men who desired other men was rarely a priority.[28] There were, in short, no 'locally inspired campaigns against homosexuals'.[29] The 'ubiquitous' use of plain-clothes officers and vice squads in parts of London to survey cruising sites such as parks and public urinals was not replicated to the same degree.[30] In Cardiff, as James Wilson explained in 1928, plain-clothes officers were used in the 'detection of indecency' but were 'not permitted to act in any sense as *agents provocateurs*'.[31] A vice squad was not established until after the Second World War.[32] Although Wilson regularly sought additional powers to deal with kerb crawling and the perceived abuse of club status to mask illegal activity, there was no desire to adopt the methods of the Metropolitan Police or the necessary infrastructure.[33] Elsewhere, the absence of plain-clothes officers, vice squads and detectives limited efficacy in this area. Even if there had been a great desire to target same-sex desire, the resources were not available.[34]

The Welsh police were different from constabularies in the north of England in one respect, namely their relative hostility to the employment of women and the use of women officers as a 'moral police force'.[35] James Wilson had a reputation for vehement opposition, and regularly lambasted the 'experiment' as a failure and a distraction from meaningful police work. He thought women physically and emotionally unfit for service.[36] As a result, there were 'no women police in Cardiff' because Wilson 'did not think police work was a women's job'. This was especially true, he believed, of sexual crimes, an area where policewomen had been employed by the northern constabularies, since 'women were not capable of dealing properly with sexual crime'.

He continued, 'no self-respecting police officer could work with police women in [such] cases ... The whole thing was revolting'.[37] Similar views were expressed by the chief constables of Glamorgan and Monmouthshire who resisted the appointment of policewomen until the 1940s.[38] In Swansea, women police were regarded as useful 'only up to a certain point'.[39] Senior police officers were supported by councillors and aldermen who made public statements such as 'can we visualise an exchange of compliments between a Bute Street virago and a policewoman?' to justify their position.[40]

According to national trends, policing of same-sex offences became more vigorous after 1945, fuelling the notion of a post-war 'heterosexual dictatorship' – a time when the state was engaged in a vigorous witch hunt against homosexuals. In that year, 223 men were charged with buggery in England and Wales, more than 1,300 with the attempt, and over 450 with gross indecency. These figures grew steadily until by the end of the decade they stood, respectively, at more than 560, 2,400, and 850.[41] Welsh cases remained, however, a tiny fraction of the whole although they did increase in this period.[42] In 1955, the chief constable of Glamorgan recorded fewer than twenty prosecutions across the three indictable categories of offence; the year before it had been just seven. Similar fluctuations were apparent in Swansea and Merthyr. Yet in Monmouthshire there was a sharp increase in arrests and prosecutions, and the county constabulary was perhaps the most active in Wales in policing same-sex offences.[43] In 1950, the county's Chief Constable, Ronald Alderson, recorded twenty seven cases; by the middle of the decade that figure had risen to more than fifty a year; and by the end of the 1950s it had more than doubled to sixty four.

Newport can be read as typical of what was going on in post-war Wales and brings into question the motif of a witch hunt and the notion of a dictatorship at the local level.[44] Arrests and prosecutions for same-sex offences peaked at eighteen a year in 1954 prompting the borough's chief constable to complain that 'crimes of violence and male indecency continue unabated'. Yet by the end of the decade the figure had fallen to fewer than half a dozen in line with data from the 1930s and the 1960s – what happened in the mid-1950s was therefore exceptional, not typical. Indeed, the Newport police were much less interested in same-sex offences than in the rising tide of teenage drunkenness and drug taking; they chose either to disregard or not to investigate the large volume of reports they received about same-sex offences and to concentrate resources elsewhere. It was true of Glamorgan, too, where scores of reports were received but few cases were actively pursued.

This cannot necessarily be seen as evidence of tolerance, of course, but it does nuance our understanding of the immediate post-war period particularly if public behaviour in reporting crime is taken to be more indicative than the police's relative lack of response. Jeffrey Weeks, who was born in the Rhondda in 1945, has argued that affluence led to 'a strengthening of narrow familiar and heterosexual values, not a liberalization of attitudes' and, therefore, 'male homosexuality [became] a target for social intervention'.[45] This is echoed by Helen Smith who has observed a sharpening of the boundaries between heterosexual and homosexual behaviour in the north of England, in contrast to the more fluid dynamics of desire apparent in the inter-war years. The more limited Welsh data also fit this pattern. In such an environment, 'homosexuality existed, but never as a distinct way of life. It was subtly crafted into the heterosexual dynamic.'[46]

Expressions of same-sex desire carried on much as before, but with increased risk, increased ostracism and increased perception of associated traits and characteristics.

Yet the 1950s did prompt a liberalising agenda: increased prosecution rates and a series of high-profile trials, most notably the Montagu case of 1954, following which the journalist Peter Wildeblood declared in his memoir 'I am a homosexual', helped to foster discussion on law reform and social equality.[47] Ahead of the 1959 general election, Roy Jenkins argued that Britain needed a campaigning home secretary to undertake the task of civilising the country. 'There is a need', he wrote, 'to create a climate of opinion which is favourable to gaiety, tolerance, and beauty, and unfavourable to puritanical restriction, to petty-minded disapproval, to hypocrisy, and to a dreary, ugly pattern of life.'[48] That process necessarily involved the implementation of the Wolfenden Committee's recommendations on decriminalising homosexuality, regardless of the hostility then found on parliamentary benches or amongst the general population. None of the Conservative government's leading members, Jenkins pointed out, 'apply social disapproval to conduct which, for public consumption, they insist on keeping subject to the full rigours of the criminal law'. He understood, as did others including Leo Abse, that British society was full of rampant hypocrisy on the question of private behaviour; hypocrisy that proved the fundamental limitations of a legal proscription which had never succeeded.

Notes

1. The following discussion of 'Fred' draws on the oral history interview published in Kevin Porter and Jeffrey Weeks, *Between the Acts: Lives of Homosexual Men, 1885–1967* (London, 1991), pp. 12–21.
2. Katherine Holden, *The Shadow of Marriage: Singleness in England, 1914–60* (Manchester, 2007), 98–9.

3. Matt Houlbrook, *Queer London: Perils and Pleasures in the Sexual Metropolis, 1918–1957* (Chicago, 2005).

4. GA, DCONMT/UNL/3, Merthyr Tydfil Constabulary, Register of Committals to Assizes, 1908–1969; GA, DCONMT/UNL/1, Merthyr Tydfil Constabulary, Crimes Register, 1924-1942.

5. *PG*, 31 May 1918.

6. *PG*, 13 January 1829; 25 May 1917; 3 September 1918.

7. *PG*, 25 February 1916.

8. *PG*, 1 November 1962.

9. *PG*, 26 January 1961.

10. Justin Bengry, 'Profit (f)or the Public Good? Sensationalism, Homosexuality, and the Postwar Popular Press', *Media History*, 20/2 (2014), 146–66.

11. *PG*, 22 July 1898.

12. *SWE*, 29 May 1894; *CT*, 14 March 1896.

13. *PG*, 22 April 1898. Codner's father, Daniel, a law graduate from Gonville and Caius College, Cambridge, held the curacy of Peterborough. His mother, Elizabeth (née Harris), was an accomplished author and magazine editor. Both were from Dartmouth in Devon. The Codner family were landed gentry and the Harris family were involved in banking. Elizabeth Codner, *Among the Brambles* (London, 1880); Codner, *Behind the Cloud* (London, 1885).

14. *CT*, 16 July 1898.

15. *The Diss Express and Norfolk and Suffolk Journal*, 31 January 1902;

16. *Eastern Daily Press*, 30 January 1902; *Norfolk Chronicle*, 1 February 1902.

17. *London Standard*, 22 November 1913.

18. *Cambria Daily Leader*, 15 April 1919.

19. I am grateful to Dr Ida Milne for her observations on this case and for suggesting the possible link between the flu epidemic and Escamilla's death. See her *Stacking the Coffins: Influenza, War and Revolution in Ireland, 1918–19* (Manchester, 2018).

20. *Herald of Wales*, 15 March 1919; *South Wales Weekly Post*, 12 April 1919.

21. GA, PSCBO/4/86: Cardiff Petty Sessions, Second Court Register, May–August 1918 – Abdulla Taslameden, 15 August 1918 (p. 280), 22 August 1918 (p. 295).

22. *PG*, 7 July 1916.

23. GA, PSCBO/4/43: Cardiff Petty Sessions, Second Court Register, December 1909–February 1910 – Louis Perlin, 11 January 1910 (pp. 155–6).

24. *South Wales Weekly Post*, 27 September 1919.

25. James Arthur Wilson was born in Yorkshire in 1877. After a brief period in the army, he joined the Barnsley Police in 1896 but quickly transferred to the Glamorgan Constabulary. Appointed Chief Constable of Merthyr Tydfil in 1908, he became Chief Constable of Cardiff in 1920 and retired in 1946. He was knighted for services to policing in 1946 and died in 1950 aged 73. Wilson proved controversial not only for his views on race but also on women – he was vehemently opposed to the introduction of women police officers (*Western Daily Press*, 24 March 1927). But he could also take a stance in support of the right of workers to fair pay (*The Stage*, 20 March 1930) and was committed to combating the development of fascism in Cardiff in the 1930s (*Aberdeen Press and Journal*, 15 October 1936).

26. *Lancashire Evening Post*, 31 January 1930.

27. *Western Gazette*, 30 November 1928.

28. Smith, *Masculinity*, p. 53. She notes that by the mid-1930s, Sheffield had 708 policemen and 6 policewomen for a city of around half a million; the Leeds force comprised 694 officers for more than 480,000 people; and in Manchester there were 1,421 officers in a city of three-quarters of a million. In Glamorgan and Monmouthshire, the average ratio was about one police officer for nearly 800 people, which translated in the Glamorgan force to an average of one officer for 824 people. Jones, *Crime and Policing in the Twentieth Century: The South Wales Experience* (Cardiff, 1996), p. 210.

29. Patrick Higgins, *Heterosexual Dictatorship: Male homosexuality in Postwar Britain* (London, 1996).

30. Houlbrook, *Queer London*, 26.

31. *The Scotsman*, 28 November 1928.

32. David J. V. Jones, *Crime and Policing in the Twentieth Century: The South Wales Experience* (Cardiff, 1996), p. 196.

33. *Western Gazette*, 30 November 1928.

34. Jones, *Crime and Policing*, p. 193; *Report from the Select Committee on Police Forces (Amalgamation)* (London: HMSO, 1932), p. 77, Q. 770; p. 137, Q. 1455A.

35. Smith, *Masculinity*, pp. 56–7. For a broader analysis of women in the police force see Louise A. Jackson, *Women Police: Gender, Welfare and Surveillance in the Twentieth Century* (Manchester, 2006).

36. *Hampshire Telegraph*, 1 April 1927.

37. *The Scotsman*, 28 November 1928.

38. Although there were a few women officers in Newport in the 1920s. *Gloucester Citizen*, 11 February 1927. For the continued resistance of the Monmouthshire Constabulary see *WM*, 22 August 1941. Likewise Flintshire: *WM*, 5 September 1940; and Breconshire: *Gloucester Citizen*, 6 July 1944.

39. *The Vote*, 4 February 1927. Although none were appointed in the city until the 1940s.

40. *Common Cause*, 19 December 1924; *The Vote*, 26 December 1924; Jones, *Crime and Policing*, p. 214.

41. These figures are based on Home Office criminal statistics reports for this period.

42. The following statistics draw on the annual reports of the Chief Constables of Glamorgan, Merthyr Tydfil, Swansea, Monmouthshire and Newport.

43. Several trials of multiple offenders were also held in Monmouthshire in this period: most notably at Abergavenny in 1942 and Usk in 1954. *News of the World*, 23 August, 8 November 1942, 13 June 1954. See also, William Cross, *The Abergavenny Witch Hunt* (Abergavenny, 2014).

44. Or, indeed, at a national level, as Matt Houlbrook has argued. *Queer London*, p. 35.

45. Weeks, *World We Have Won*, p. xi.

46. As n.45, p. 31.

47. Peter Wildeblood, *Against the Law* (London, 1955).

48. Roy Jenkins, *The Labour Case* (London, 1959).

PART TWO

Coming Together

CHAPTER THREE

Seeking Love, Finding It

In 1972, Malcolm, a young man in his mid-twenties living in
Aberystwyth, placed an advert in the classified section of *Gay
News*. He described himself as 'sincere, non-effeminate [and]
seeking similar male in twenties, anywhere (preferably with own
pad) for permanent friendship, with a view to living together'.[1]
Another advertiser, who was from Carmarthenshire and in his
late forties, complained of being lonely but otherwise described
himself as having a 'sturdy build' and as 'non-effeminate, [and]
sincere'.[2] Both adverts were clear invitations for male companionship at a time when the prospects of meeting other gay people
were relatively slim. Indeed, when he received no reply to his
initial advert, Malcolm subsequently reflected in a follow-up that
he was 'tired of being alone' and was 'in need of love'.[3] This
was a common experience. The personal ads placed in friendly
newspapers and magazines were a vital way of breaking through
silences and absences. Others used the relative anonymity of the
classifieds to express their true identities, as these adverts illustrate: 'West Midlands/Welsh border. Married man but completely
gay (43) but young and active, desperate for gay love and companionship weekends. Letters welcome.' And: 'Married male (gay)

non-effeminate, wishes to meet similar South Wales/Bristol.'[4] The closer to urban centres one lived, the closer one was to the few gay clubs and pubs that existed in the late 1960s and early 1970s, the less powerful feelings of loneliness were. Adverts placed by those living in Cardiff, for instance, were much more adventurous than those in rural areas and sought to cultivate companionship based on similar interests or physical appearance. The following advert, placed in the alternative newspaper *International Times* in March 1969, was typical: 'CARDIFF area: young man (22) would like to meet good-looking males of same age.'[5] Similar adverts appeared in *Gay News*, in sympathetic journals such as *Marxism Today* or *Spare Rib*, and in international gay magazines especially in North America.[6] In 1984, one Cardiff man in his early thirties wrote to *Body Politic* in Toronto saying he 'needs more from life with that special someone' and was willing to relocate for the right partner.[7]

It is easy to imagine that these kinds of public appeals were part of the increasing visibility of lesbians and gay men after 1967, and that the freedom provided by gay-orientated newspapers and magazines or gay-friendly ones started this kind of semi-public conversation. Or that it had never existed before. But this assumption all too easily disguises several generations of more carefully coded use of classified advertisement columns and magazine illustration.[8] Like all secret messages, they take a degree of patience and supposition to read accurately, but once unlocked the homophile appeal is immediately apparent. Adverts were initially written in such a way as to appear innocuous, run-of-the-mill, everyday. But, of course, they were not. Examples appeared in the *Western Mail*, the *South Wales Echo* and the Cardiff *Evening Express* in the 1890s and early 1900s. For instance: 'Young gentleman would like to share his bed and sitting room with another: hot and cold bath. 25, Moira Terrace.'[9] Or: 'A respectable young man would like another to share his bed and sitting room: hot and cold bath, 45 Talworth Street, Roath.'[10] Or: 'To bachelors only – gentleman, young, desires share quarters with another, not under forty, in Cardiff; companionship chief consideration – write fully and confidentially.'[11] Or, 'Bachelor, having house at Llanishen would like another to share. Trains very convenient.'[12]

Victorian and Edwardian Cardiffians certainly shared digs because it was a city where rented accommodation was much in demand: just before the First World War more than one-third of families lived in houses of multiple occupation and there was continuous subdivision of dwellings to make housing more affordable.[13] To that end, this kind of advert was relatively straightforward, common even, and the columns of newspapers were full of adverts from landlords offering rooms to would-be tenants and from would-be tenants seeking rooms or people to share with. But clearly these were carefully worded advertisements, telling the right kind of gentleman bachelor what he needed to know. The later classified adverts in gay magazines descended from these coded ancestors.

Compared with London-based journals such as *The Link*, whose lonely-hearts columns provided cover for homosexual correspondence and social engagement, the adverts which appeared in Cardiff newspapers were often cautious, even timid: about sharing rooms rather than social or cultural interests. No one declared themselves, as did one correspondent of *The Link* in 1920, 'artistic [and a] firm believer in [Edward] Carpenter's books', nor did they dare explain that they had been 'looking for many years for [a] tall, manly Hercules'.[14] Women's voices were especially absent, although they were not in metropolitan magazines. Yet in Cardiff's reading rooms and public libraries, as well as through newsagents and individual subscriptions, women and men had ready access to the homoerotic and homosocial literature of the metropolis. One such journal was *The Artist and Journal of Home Culture*, a sixpenny monthly which has attracted the attention of several historians for its clear attempt to 'establish a visible gay discourse, a gay tradition, and a gay interpretative community of readers before 1895 and the [Oscar] Wilde trials'.[15] Nor was *The Artist* unique in promoting the homoerotic ideals of classical masculine beauty, with art magazines such as *The Studio* and *The Yellow Book* offering similar kinds of material.

Under editor Charles Kains Jackson, who took up the post in around 1888, *The Artist* accommodated a considerable variety of gay material often pseudonymously or anonymously depending on how explicit it was, although the absence of illustration was probably the journal's saving grace: homoerotic subtext could be usefully ignored, imagery could not be. Nevertheless, 'few reading *The Artist* regularly ... could remain unaware of this [homosexual] strain.' According to its register of subscriptions, Cardiff library was subscribed to *The Artist* by 1890 and maintained its subscription until the journal ceased publication in 1902.[16] Therefore, all of Kains Jackson's efforts to produce a gay discourse in its pages were available to read with no attempt at censorious action (such as cancelling the subscription) undertaken either by the staff or the council's library committee. Similarly, much was made in *The Artist* of Michelangelo, particularly the two-volume biography produced by J. A. Symonds, whose writing has long been regarded as conveying gay discourse, in which the Renaissance artist's relationship with Tommaso dei Cavalieri was established as homosexual. Given this enthusiasm, the donation of a marble replica of Michelangelo's 'David' to Cardiff Museum and Art

Gallery in 1898 no doubt provided further opportunities for the exercise of a queer gaze.[17]

Although much of the most overtly gay material which made up the 'pink market niche' came from, and was centred around, elements of London society fascinated by continental Europe and classical artistic forms which championed the naked male form, it had a resonance, however small, in Cardiff. In fact, the following carefully observed passage from *The Athenaeum* on George Borrow, author of *Wild Wales*, clearly borrowed from the Kains Jackson tradition of eroticised Hellenism and gay subjectivity. It was first published in 1899 but was reprinted in the *Public Library Journal*, a magazine produced jointly by Cardiff Free Libraries and Penarth Public Library, in 1901:

> Standing considerably above six feet in height, he was built as perfectly as a Greek statue, and his practice of athletic exercises gave his every movement the easy elasticity of an athlete under training ... the silvery whiteness of the thick crop of hair seemed to add in a remarkable way to the beauty of the hairless face.[18]

Thus, discourse which had had prominence in the early 1890s, and which suffered considerably from censorship and proscription in the middle of the decade, began to reappear at the turn of the century albeit more cautiously in its traversal of the fine line between unacceptable homoeroticism and acceptable aestheticism. Classical and Renaissance art, which was widely regarded as a legitimate object of academic study, otherwise meant that in museums, art galleries and libraries the 'observer was free to look ... unhindered by the complicated array of discourses the city street outside might evoke'.[19]

Public art was separate from private or commercial exhibition and the latter ran the risk of outraging prevailing sensibilities. In 1896, an exhibitor of 'French Fine Art' (in practice, erotic pictures of naked women) based in Castle Street, Cardiff, was raided by police and several of the images were seized. According to the testimony of the detective who conducted the case, he had paid a penny to a thirteen year old boy to enter the exhibition and another penny to enter the 'for gentlemen only' exhibition at the rear. The case was dismissed, however, when magistrates noted that the photographs were no more risqué than those seen in London studios.[20] A similar exhibition was targeted in Swansea a few years earlier.[21] One local newspaper took aim at the prudish members of the National Vigilance Association, which aimed at the repression of vice and public immorality, and remarked that 'the nude is not always rude'.[22] Another observed that

> penny peep shows are not, as a rule, the most elevating of public exhibitions, but their owners should enjoy the same rights and privileges as are permitted to be extended to the proprietors of picture galleries and museums ... If the nude or semi-nude in art be really indecent, it is equally so from whatever point of view regarded – whether represented at an itinerant show, or depicted on canvas, carved in stone, or produced in the *Magazine of Art* or any other periodical ... it requires an impure mind to conjure up all manner of imaginary indecencies from representations of the human form.[23]

Technological innovations by the end of the nineteenth century enabled exhibitors to display images by means of a penny slot machine, some of which were 'artistic' nudes, others involved cats in amusing situations.[24]

Few people needed to go to an art gallery, museum, public library or peep show to see naked bodies. They were a common sight, especially in periods of hot weather when swimming in the lakes and rivers was widespread. Councillors complained, to little effect not least because as many people stood and watched as felt discomfort, of the 'great deal of nuisance ... occasioned to people in the district by persons bathing in the river ... and running about the roads in a naked state'.[25] Underground, men took off as many clothes as were necessary to work in the sweltering conditions of the pit; and at home the tin bath in front of the fire hardly occasioned the privacy of twenty-first century bathrooms. This familiarity with the body together with the physically taxing nature of industrial work and its economic precariousness meant that working-class people had 'little time or inclination to worry about how pleasure was sought'.[26] But where did men and women go to meet potential partners?

One of the rare instances in which the police were called because a couple were spotted having sex, and which therefore provides a direct glimpse at the geography of same-sex desire, took place in Merthyr Tydfil towards the end of the Second World War. A young soldier, home on leave, was found with an older man in his early fifties 'lying on the floor at the rear of the Pant Baths, Dowlais, one lying on his stomach with his trousers down, the other lying on top of him with clothes disarranged'. Those involved were sentenced to as much as a year's hard labour in prison. The soldier never returned to active service. A similar incident, also from Merthyr, took place a few years earlier when the police caught a man 'putting his person between [another man's] legs'. The 'perpetrator' was sentenced to three months' hard labour. By the early 1960s, cars were also favoured as places in which sexual activity could be enjoyed; one incident from Tonyrefail, which the police dismissed as likely made up, recorded that 'a man ... had indecently assaulted [the teenager] by masturbating him in his car'. Whether made up or not in this instance, it was hardly an unlikely occurrence.

'Cruising' for same-sex partners took place everywhere from mountainsides to railway carriages, from public toilets to dockland lodging houses and from cinemas to swimming baths: as a direct consequence of their use as places for 'picking people up' public toilets took on the guise of the 'cottage'.[27] There were implicit rules and signals which indicated whether a person was present for a hook-up or simply to urinate.[28] In the Valleys, relatively isolated hillsides provided a similar function.[29] For much of the 1970s and early 1980s, part of Jersey Marine beach near Swansea was adopted as a gay beach, and Newport had its own gay sauna.[30] The streets, of course, were the most important cruising space, where nods, winks and lingering glances transformed interactions between strangers into something more deliberate. Those who cruised relied on the inclination of most people to ignore anything more than the most overt of differences, and in the hustle and bustle of busy streets it was easier to mask social practices otherwise regarded as deviant. Whereas the streets were a place of solicitation, they could not be used safely for sexual activity and as a result a range of semi-private spaces became venues into which gays and lesbians (or those willing to have some form of same-sex encounter) retreated.

Given the relatively late development of overt gay nightlife, cruising practices developed in the late nineteenth century lasted until the end of the twentieth particularly (though not exclusively) in the southern coalfield and in rural areas. As one observer wrote of Ceredigion and rural Carmarthenshire in 1972, 'from what I have seen, there appears to be considerable "cottage" activity even in the wildest areas in that part of Wales.'[31] In 1982, the international gay guide *Spartacus* noted that there appeared 'to be a lot of cottaging in the industrial valleys'.[32] In the 1980s, councillors in Aberystwyth received regular complaints that the town's public toilets were 'being used for gay sex sessions'.[33] The toilets in Newport Bus Station were often used by men travelling into the city from the Monmouthshire Valleys, with those in the town's leisure centre frequented by local residents; and researchers for Project Sigma focused their efforts on a series of cottaging sites in Cardiff, including several locations in Bute Park and at public toilets in Cathays Park and Cardiff Central Station.[34]

If toilets, the streets and other semi-public places fitted with the urban geographies of anonymous sex identified elsewhere, several of the instances recorded in the police and court records clearly point to the role of the workplace in providing working-class men, especially, with opportunities to have sex with other men whom they knew. What else to make of incidents occurring between young men in dairies, garages, railway stations, building sites and so forth; or between labourers and colliers and railway-men? In recognising that same-sex desire was not only expressed in places of entertainment or on the streets but in places of work, too, we can nuance prevailing assumptions about masculinity, gender and prejudice. Although it was understood in the early part of the twentieth century that 'the working class was not particularly bothered by homosexuality', that did not mean that all working-class men were comfortable with having sex or engaging in a romantic relationship with another man.[35] Nevertheless, too sharp a distinction can be made between a masculinity which prized its physicality, strength and good character, and which also displayed an ambivalence to ostensibly criminalised sexual behaviour or gender diversity.

This was the case in Merthyr Tydfil, where a local 'character' proved the extent of working-class tolerance of difference alongside physical prowess. With his broad shoulders and, at least as photographs from the late 1970s and early 1980s show him, round figure and jowls, Billy Pugh (1900–1984) was similar in stature and physique to many older men from the Valleys. As a young man he had worked as a blacksmith at the Ivor Works in Dowlais, but following the demise of the industry got a job as a binman on the Corporation refuse lorry. He retained the physical strength gained from heavy industrial labour and could carry two bins, one over each shoulder. Much of the time, at least in the day, Billy Pugh travelled around Merthyr Tydfil and Dowlais on the lorry in his council uniform of blue boiler suit and black T-shirt; hardly different from his colleagues. But if residents looked more carefully, they noticed the make-up on Billy Pugh's face, the lipstick, coloured polish on his fingernails, and women's stockings under his overalls. His hair, too, was dyed black, albeit in later years he had greying temples. On days off, it might be contained in a hair net like that worn by the iconic Coronation Street character Ena Sharples, played by Violet Carson.

In the evenings, Billy Pugh often performed in drag in the workingmen's clubs, pubs and hotel lounges of Merthyr Tydfil and Dowlais, adopting the stage name Teacher Bessie (although in more upmarket settings he worked under the guise of Madame Sonia). One of his favoured songs was Arthur Askey's double-entendre-laden Second World War classic 'I want a banana', and he produced similarly suggestive alternative lyrics for more contemporary hits such as Boney M's 'Brown girl in the ring'. In his study of the *Real Merthyr*, journalist Mario Basini, whose parents ran an Italian café in the town frequented by the town's binmen amongst others, reflected that it was 'a measure of the humanity of "Macho Merthyr" that [Billy Pugh's] presence in the town was accepted with amused tolerance and understanding. He never, as far as I know, provoked persecution or even mild condemnation'.[36] There were stares, of course, especially from the curious but these were met with a resolute look of disapproval or contempt, and stares were not repeated a second time; there was nothing overtly homophobic said to him. Billy Pugh was not entirely unique, and there were similar individuals in Cardiff and elsewhere who lived as they wished to live, challenged expectations, and ensured, through quiet dignity at work, raucous innuendo at play, and above all immense bravery, that not only was working-class sexual diversity apparent, and visible, it was accepted as part of day-to-day life. As one man observed in 1969,

> Most of our friends know what our relationship is, accept it as normal and I don't think I have heard any stupid comment for a long time. There used to be a few people who thought it was funny or clever to make the sort of two-side comment which sets the ignorant rolling with smutty laughter, but I think that, at last, people are beginning to grow up.[37]

Media portraits and memoirs of working-class homosexuality in Wales in the 1960s and 1970s, and beyond, have tended to point the other way. Integration, which was apparent, sat uneasily with the more widely circulated (and therefore assumed) narrative of exclusion and ostracism. Hence an interview published in the *South Wales Echo* in 1971 with a 'tall, fairly hefty forestry worker' called Andrew. He was in his early thirties, lived with his mother in a Monmouthshire village, had short hair (in contrast to the long hair which was 'expected' of all deviant members of society at that time) and was 'well spoken'. But, the newspaper reported, because he was a gay bachelor Andrew did not feel part of society; instead he felt 'like a leper' and unable to settle into a community that did not fully accept him.[38] Even gay activists worried that unsuspecting family members might find material sent to them by organisations such as the Campaign for Homosexual Equality and complained about the poor quality of envelopes used for correspondence, and most gay magazines explained to subscribers that they would be sent in plain packaging.

In rural areas, where arrests and court cases were rare and attitudes assumed to be more conservative, there was inevitably less visibility – hence the frequency of cottaging – but there was also a different rhythm to gay life from that found in urban areas. The Gay Rural Aid and Information Network (GRAIN), which was established in 1976, was an ostensibly national organisation, but its primary roots – and, from 1980, its administrative headquarters – were in Colwyn Bay. GRAIN advertised itself as 'for gays into crafts, self-sufficiency or just rural living' and was intended by its London-based founders as a support organisation for gays and lesbians living in isolated areas providing an exchange of information and instruction in relevant rural skills. In other words, a means of fitting in with the rural way of life as much as possible, but also avoiding the need to rely entirely on the 'unsympathetic and often hostile heterosexual community'.[39] It eventually consisted of 'a heterogeneous mix of lesbian and gay environmentalists and "back-to-the-land" enthusiasts, older lesbians and gay men who had retired to the countryside, and rural-based gay activists'.[40]

Instead of organising trips to gay pubs and clubs, as was the case with urban support groups, members of GRAIN were taken to the Centre for Alternative Technology in Machynlleth (which sold various gay magazines and newspapers), they linked up with branches of the Campaign for Nuclear Disarmament, advertised in CND's newspaper *Peace News*, and debated the importance of self-sufficiency, sustainable production, environmentalism and the future of the planet. They 'engaged in all sorts of non-waged labour, domestic production, bartering and skill-swaps', and rejected entirely the commercial orientation of 'mainstream', even 'normal, gay life in large towns and cities.[41] In this way, the gay back-to-the-land movement was a novel fusion of sexual politics, green politics, language politics and at times a conservative rejection of contemporary ways of living, both in a hetero- and homonormative sense. Whether or not it took inspiration from television series such as *The Good Life*, which first aired in April 1975 and shone an amusing light onto urban flight into the countryside, this was a moment of diverse organisation within the gay movement which resonated in those parts of Britain normally forgotten about.

Perhaps the fullest expression of a homosexual and homosocial back-to-the-land movement was the 'wimmin's land' established in Lampeter towards the end of the 1970s. Inspired by a visit to the Oregon Women's Land, which was set up in 1976, and by Jill Johnston's 1973 book *Lesbian Nation*, the founders of the Lampeter community aimed at a full rejection of paternalism and male-dominated capitalist society: what became known eventually as lesbian separatism. In such environments men and boys were entirely absent and women were encouraged to find solutions to problems in their own way through consciousness raising and the implementation of the most radical ideas of women's liberation. The Lampeter wimmin's land formed part of an international network linking not only Oregon but also women's intentional communities elsewhere in the United States,

New South Wales, and Denmark. Women travelled to and from the communities as part of what Rebecca Jennings has called 'lesbian circuits of mobility' sharing feminist ideas and ways of living. These principles also found their way into other aspects of life in Lampeter, not least the all-woman Ragged Robin clothing co-operative which was founded in 1979 and produced and sold clothing for women through mail order and by advertising in feminist magazines including *Spare Rib*. It survived until 1984, but inspired several other women's co-operatives including the Happy Hands Women's Sewing Co-operative in Port Talbot and the Marged Women's Shoe Co-operative in Llanddewi Brefi.[42]

These links illustrated that although rural Wales attracted many of the more radical approaches to feminist organisation, such ideas were also apparent in the Valleys, too, particularly as those communities were confronted with the post-industrial dilemma of the 1970s and 1980s. Situated high on the hillside overlooking Pontypridd and the lower Rhondda, Lan Farm offered idyllic views and the country lanes which led to the Llanwonno Forestry were (and remain) popular with cyclists and walkers. Towards the end of the 1980s, the farm was bought by two lesbians who set about turning it into a hostel exclusively for gay men and women seeking peace and quiet far enough away from the city, but not too far.[43] As one travel guide put it, the hostel was 'located on a big, big hill between Cardiff and the Brecon Beacons National Park' and offered a 'traditional Welsh farmhouse with cozy fireplace and sitting room surrounded by a meadow with panoramic views'.[44] Lan Farm may not have offered the full back-to-the-land experience but in its own way it reproduced a quasi-rural existence and provided a queer hostelry in a town that otherwise had very little sign of active lesbian and gay life.

The radical movements of the 1970s believed in the essential necessity of consciousness raising to forge new identities, whether feminist, black or queer. Coming out, argued the Gay Liberation Front in its manifesto, was the first (political) step taken by gay men and women in transforming themselves and raising awareness and understanding of what it meant to be homosexual. 'By freeing our heads', they argued, 'we get the confidence to come out publicly and proudly as gay people, and to win over our gay brothers and sisters to the ideas of gay liberation.'[45] It was not enough simply to cruise parks and toilets for sex and otherwise eschew a gay identity; rather, gay people should adopt a liberated lifestyle free of the established norms of society including marriage, family and even monogamy. Thus, in parts of London, notably Brixton, the squat and gay centres opened in unoccupied buildings became a central feature of efforts to create queer alternatives to 'mainstream' ways of living. As Matt Cook has observed,

> The communards especially tried to jettison notions of privacy, private property, and monogamy and to provide a counter to the nuclear home and family which they saw embedding sexism, homophobia, and capitalism, and inhibiting self-expression and exploration.[46]

But outside London, this type of squat and this type of behaviour was much less common. In Cardiff, a survey of seventeen squats undertaken by the city's Housing Action Group in 1976 found that more than three-quarters were occupied by people with children who had, for various reasons, not been provided with accommodation by the council.[47]

The idea of coming out, though, did take hold, together with the encouragement to love oneself and to be proud. Coming-out

narratives were powerful testimony of growing self-awareness
and re-fashioning of personal identity. Some illustrated strength
of conviction, others the complexities of understanding and self-
confidence. Writing in the pages of *Seren*, the student newspaper
at UCNW in Bangor, one young man reflected on the process:

> I arrived in Bangor a determined 18 year old. I was deter-
> mined to come to terms with my sexuality, confident that
> in an academic environment such as this it wouldn't matter
> to anyone who I found sexually attractive. Well, it took this
> determined 18 year old over a year to do what he'd intended
> to do in his first week here.[48]

In another, lengthier article, another student told of how

> I'd had what could be termed as quite a 'comfortable' edu-
> cation, straight from a pleasant Catholic sixth form in a
> comfortable part of the country ... Imagine my reaction, as
> I came to the conclusion that I was rather more attracted
> to the boys in my class than the girls, when our Religious
> education teacher informed us that homosexuals were not
> to be seen as equal in the eyes of God as 'normal' people,
> and that homosexuality, like masturbation, was a sin ... I felt
> isolated, and had no one to talk things over with, I couldn't
> tell my parents ... I couldn't tell my friends ... I certainly
> couldn't tell my priest!

He came to university 'tight-lipped and with a secret to hide'. At
fresher's fayre, he kept a distance from the GaySoc stall for fear
of upsetting the friendships that he had begun to forge in halls.
He continued:

I settled down well in my little room ... and settled down into college routine. We'd normally go to as many discos and events as possible, the work ethic not being exactly ingrown in us, and occasionally I'd see posters for activities concerning the Lesbian and Gay Group and wonder what they were like, and how many people went to them and if any of the men wore dresses, but by now my feet were quite firmly entrenched in a 'straight' set of friends.

To ease his transition out of the closet, he told his friends that he was bisexual and moved on quickly from the announcement with little real impact on their friendship. When a school friend came out in a letter and a close friend at Bangor did the same, 'I came to a decision, gay men were no longer vague shadows on the horizons.' He went along to GaySoc and 'for the first time I was able to meet with and talk to a group of people like myself and I felt as if a weight had been taken off my shoulders.' He concluded: 'That was a year and a half ago. Since then I've learnt a lot, both through the group and outside it, the most important thing being I can now hold my head up and say to myself 'I am gay' without any feelings of guilt or self-recrimination.'[49]

Similar coming-out stories were published in the student press elsewhere, notably in Cardiff. During the university's Gay Awareness Week in 1987, *Gair Rhydd* published an article from Henry, who reflected that

Realising that I was gay was never a problem, doing something about it was. Before coming to College, the only knowledge I had of lesbians and gay men, if you can call it that, was that handed out [by] the press, TV and friends. All

lesbians were butch and men-haters and gays were limp-
wristed and effeminate.

Public statements of this kind were intended to encourage others
in the university who were gay to come out and to join the gay
movement. For most, however, coming out was semi-private
with advice sought from sympathetic friends, dedicated organisations such as CHE, and telephone befriending services such
as Switchboard, Icebreakers, FRIEND and the lesbian lines established in Swansea at the end of 1979, Cardiff in October 1981, and
Bangor by the spring of 1984.[50] With strong links to women's
liberation and the women's aid movement, the lesbian lines were
endowed with a clear understanding of the need to wrest organisation of lesbian activity from the other largely male-orientated gay
institutions. 'Due to the nature of our work', noted Cardiff Lesbian
Line in 1983, 'male administrators of money don't give us any.'[51]

Cardiff FRIEND was established in 1973 as part of an expansion of the service from London to regional centres notably
Birmingham, Brighton, Cambridge, Manchester and Liverpool,
and was initially based at an office in St Mary's Street before moving to longer-term headquarters in Charles Street.[52] The first calls
were taken on 25 September and included several men who were
either married or divorced and an Irishman who wanted to learn
a bit more about the gay scene in the city.[53] They were typical of
the early days of the service – volunteers provided advice about
venues to visit, where to buy gay magazines and to meet other
people; some also asked for information about 'cures'. Many of
the most challenging (but rewarding) calls were about coming
out and about the isolation felt by those living in the Valleys.
One teenager ringing in the late 1970s explained how he had
seen television programmes such as *The Naked Civil Servant* and

items on the news which gave him the awareness that he was gay; but with no other gay people at school and limited access to information, he felt isolated and alone. The log book recorded that 'he felt much better for having a talk'.

Other callers were in their twenties and speaking to others about their feelings for the first time, as was the case for one man from the Rhymney Valley. Living at home with his parents, he was concerned about their hostile attitudes towards gay people and about being discovered, but nevertheless he felt he had 'bottled things up for too long'. It was likewise for a striking miner who rang FRIEND in the summer of 1984. Having thus far lived a 'discrete lifestyle' connected to gay people only by means of a friendship circle in the Rhymney Valley, he knew little about the wider culture or available sources of information including *Gay News*. FRIEND provided him with a means of coming out 'a bit more', and encouraged stronger engagement with what was going on in Cardiff. Other miners, soldiers and men from ethnic minorities rang with similar questions and in similar predicaments. One miner from the Rhondda, who told volunteers he was both bisexual and gay during their conversation, explained that his wife knew about his homosexuality but they never discussed it. Instead, he sought the companionship of men outside the Rhondda, but 'because of the distance to Newport and Cardiff he [hadn't] been able to sustain them.'

Advice lines were used not only by those who were gay themselves, or questioning their sexuality, but also by distressed parents worried about their children or the reaction of their spouses and their families, or by equally concerned siblings worried about promiscuous behaviour. One mother rang FRIEND in 1988 to discuss a delicate situation at home: her eldest son had recently come out and her younger son 'has [a] strong suspicion that he is gay'. She blamed herself for both of her sons being gay but could find little direct evidence in their upbringing as to why it should be so. Instead she reflected on the fact her husband had 'rejected the older one when he found out and has always threatened the younger one if he caused any upset'. The worry and the anguish, particularly about familial violence which was a relatively common concern, was poured out over the telephone and then through dedicated parental advice services and support groups as a follow-up. The lack of state-funded programmes meant that these were provided by volunteers from FRIEND, CHE and the Rights and Information Bureau in Charles Street.

Ultimately, what callers to advice services most often wanted was a gay social life and the means of breaking out of isolation or out of the habits of cottaging and cruising, because they were married and felt they had no choice. Those who volunteered to operate the telephones became experts on the various gay bars and clubs and the branches of CHE that existed around the country to answer questions about where to go – either because the caller lived in a particular place or because they were visiting for work or a holiday. For the youngest, a telephone call or the support of the befriending service was a vital means of coming to terms with sexuality, as one young man from Barry found when he met with volunteers from FRIEND who introduced him to the gay scene in Cardiff. On their first meeting, the group discussed the young man's life, his aspirations and his feelings. He told them that he had never been attracted to girls and had been a rugby player until 'his frustration at seeing the men getting changed became too great'. On a second visit, the group went to the Terminus, although the young man found that unnerving, and instead they settled at the more comfortable King's Cross. Eventually, the young man found his place in gay Cardiff abandoning the 'training wheels' of the befriending service. As was recorded in the FRIEND log,

> I didn't see him then again until I bumped into him propping up the bar there [at the Terminus] last Monday. He seemed happy and contented to chat to his neighbour. I think he is as well together as any of us and should not be molly coddled. His mother seems quite liberal.

Befrienders understood that there were differences between the gay venues both in Cardiff and more generally and were careful when meeting people new to the scene to start at the King's Cross and move on from there. Bars and clubs, rather than cafes or advice centres or bookshops, became the heart of gay Wales: places to seek love and friendship and to find it.

Notes

1. *GN*, 14 September 1972.
2. *GN*, 24 January 1973.
3. *GN*, 24 January 1973.
4. Both were placed in *GN*, 21 February 1973.
5. *International Times*, 51 (28 February–13 March 1969).
6. See the advert placed by CHE Swansea and Neath in *Body Politic* (Toronto) in November 1976; *Spare Rib*, 120 (July 1982).
7. *Body Politic* (November 1984; November 1986).
8. H. G. Cocks, *Classified: The Secret History of the Personal Column* (London, 2009).
9. *SWE*, 27 November 1895; *EEx*, 17 January 1896.
10. *SWE*, 12 November 1896.
11. *WM*, 4 October 1900.
12. *EEx*, 18 June 1904.
13. Martin Daunton, *Coal Metropolis: Cardiff, 1870–1914* (Leicester, 1977); M. J. Daunton, *House and Home in the Victorian City: Working-Class Housing, 1850–1914* (London, 1983).

14. *The Link* (September 1920). Cited in H. G. Cocks, '"Sporty" Girls and "Artistic" Boys: Friendship, Illicit Sex, and the British "Companionship" Advertisement, 1913–1928', *Journal of the History of Sexuality*, 11/3 (2002), 457–482.

15. Laurel Brake, *Print in Transition, 1850-1910: Studies in Media and Book History* (London, 2001), 142; Matt Cook, *London and the Culture of Homosexuality, 1885–1914* (Cambridge, 2003), pp. 127–9.

16. Cardiff Free Libraries, Museum and Art Gallery, *Twenty Ninth Annual Report* (Cardiff, 1891), pp. 30–1.

17. Cardiff Museum and Art Gallery, *Report for the Year Ending 31 October 1898* (Cardiff, 1898), p. 15.

18. *The Athenaeum*, 25 March 1899; reprinted in *The Public Library Journal*, 3/2 (Cardiff, March 1901), 45.

19. Matthew David Cook, 'The inverted city: London and the constitution of homosexuality, 1885–1914' (unpublished Ph.D. thesis, Queen Mary University of London, 2000), 192.

20. *EEx*, 25 March 1896.

21. *CT*, 15 December 1894.

22. *EEx*, 26 March 1896.

23. *The Cambrian*, 14 December 1894.

24. *EEx*, 24 April 1899.

25. *SWDN*, 14 June 1895.

26. Smith, *Masculinity*, 127.

27. *Western Daily Press*, 12 July 1978.

28. Alan John Butler, 'Performing LGBT Pride in Plymouth, 1950-2012' (unpublished Ph.D. thesis, Plymouth University, 2015), 56; Matt Houlbrook, 'The Private World of Public Urinals: London, 1918–57', *The London Journal*, 25/1 (2000), 52–70.

29. *EEx*, 22 March 1898.

30. *Broadsheet* (Leeds), 12 (December 1972).

31. LSE Archives, Hall-Carpenter Collection, CHE Records, HCA/CHE/7/153: 'Letter from Derrick Stephens to Peter Temperton, 20 February 1972'.

32. *Spartacus International Gay Guide* (New York, 1982), p. 815.

33. *WM*, 12 February 1988.

34. A P. M. Coxon, *Between the Sheets: Sexual Diaries and Gay Men's Sex in the Era of AIDS* (London, 1996), p. 6.

35. Jeffrey Weeks, *Coming Out* (London, 1977), p. 40; Smith, *Masculinity*, p. 95.

36. Mario Basini, *Real Merthyr* (Bridgend, 2009), pp. 90–1.

37. *WM*, 17 June 1969, cited in Martin Johnes, *Wales since 1939* (Manchester, 2011), p. 350.

38. *SWE*, 15 September 1971.

39. *Spare Rib*, 181 (August 1987), 56.

40. Gavin Brown, 'Rethinking the Origins of Homonormativity: The Diverse Economies of Rural Gay Life in England and Wales in the 1970s and 1980s', *Transactions of the Institute of British Geographers*, 40/4 (2015), 549–61.

41. Gavin Brown, 'Before same-sex marriage: finding "homonormativity" in rural Wales in the early 1980s'. Available online: *https://blog. geographydirections.com/2015/09/08/before-same-sex-marriage-finding-homonormativity-in-rural-wales-in-the-early-1980s/* (accessed: 5 July 2018).

42. *Spare Rib*, 120 (July 1982), 37–8; *Lampeter Grapevine* 20 (June 2014), 6–7.

43. *Spare Rib*, 190 (May 1988), 35; Miranda Davies and Natania Jansz, *Women Travel: Adventures, Advice and Experience* (London, 1994), p. 80.

44. Lindsy van Gelder and Pamela Robin Brandt, *Are You Two ... Together? A Gay and Lesbian Travel Guide to Europe* (London, 1991), p. 57.

45. Gay Liberation Front, *Manifesto* (London, 1971).

46. Matt Cook, '"Gay Times": Identity, Locality, Memory, and the Brixton Squats in 1970s London', *Twentieth Century British History*, 24/1 (2013), 84–109.

47. Cardiff Housing Action Group, *Before You Open Your Big Mouth: A Report on Squatting by Cardiff Housing Action* (Cardiff, 1976).

48. *Seren*, 21 April 1986.

49. *Seren*, 4 November 1985.

50. *Spare Rib*, 90 (January 1980), 28; *Spare Rib*, 140 (March 1984), 32.

51. *Cardiff Women's Liberation Magazine* (December 1983). The service had been established in October 1981 and was based at the Women's Centre in Coburn Street. *Cardiff Women's Liberation Magazine* (July 1981; October 1981).

52. *GN*, 7 March 1973. The north Wales equivalent was established in Llandudno in 1977 by members of CHE Gwynedd. Prior to its creation calls had been directed to the Merseyside service or to Cardiff. CHE Gwynedd, Newssheet, 13 (April 1977).

53. This section draws on a close reading of the surviving logbooks of Cardiff FRIEND held at the Glamorgan Archives and provides a representative sample of the information contained therein. As they are not yet fully catalogued, and to preserve the anonymity of the entries, I have refrained from providing complete references.

CHAPTER FOUR

Dancing the Night Away

In 1939, a survey of London dance halls recorded a conversation with a Welshman who had been spotted dancing with other men. Although this was common in the metropolis, the observer assumed that men from the provinces who danced with each other were effeminate or had latent homosexual tendencies. But, he was told that men dancing with other men was a regular occurrence in the Valleys, and some were so used to 'taking the lady's part' that they struggled to revert to leading when dancing with women.[1] With its largely middle-class cohort of survey takers and observers, Mass Observation was often surprised at the fluid notions of masculinity amongst industrial workers and their willingness to ignore 'boundaries' established by bourgeois taste and decency. Indeed, in one scene from a Lambeth dance hall published in the 1939 Penguin Special, *Britain*, mass observers witnessed a series of 'lewd' pantomimes, with working-class men dressed up in women's clothes (complete with false breasts) dancing with each other, swearing, and making suggestive gestures of sexual performance.

Nor were such amusements limited to London. In urban parts of Wales, there was a small network of coffee shops, pubs, dance halls and cinemas where it was understood that men could socialise together without concerning themselves about desire and its implications. Venues which subsequently attracted working-class gay men were often those which had always been 'neither glamorous nor politicised but the province of ... outsiders' and were rarely exclusive to a gay clientele.[2] They had a record of being denounced by the police and magistrates as venues where drinking was taken to excess and where prostitutes were either active in selling their services or sought refuge from the streets. In the late nineteenth century, the licensee at the Terminus, which became one of the more prominent gay bars in the 1980s, was fined twice for 'permitting his premises to be the resort of prostitutes by allowing them to remain longer than was necessary for refreshment' and charged with (though not prosecuted for) serving drunkards. The Golden Cross, the York Hotel and the Royal Hotel had similar histories; each was recognised as gay-friendly in the 1970s.

The purpose of this chapter, then, is to establish the social spaces in Cardiff and elsewhere in which same-sex desire and companionship were expressed during the nineteenth and twentieth centuries – a range of venues intended for socialising rather than cruising, although the latter was never absent. Whereas a commercial gay scene did emerge in the 1970s, for the most part these venues were integrated into working-class male culture and used for a variety of purposes. This remained the case until at least the Second World War when pubs slowly became more accommodating of women as customers, although private members' clubs remained homosocial well into the 1980s, with women actively refused entry. This distinction was also apparent in the development of a gay scene which appealed chiefly to men and had a 'macho' image unappealing to lesbians and transgender men and women. There have, trad-itionally, been fewer venues aimed at those parts of the LGBT community.

Before the advent of the modern nightclub in the early 1960s, it was the pub, the dance hall, the coffee tavern or lodging house that provided opportunities for working-class men to meet other men. James Steele, a thirty-year-old sailor, was arrested in January 1892 for having committed an 'abominable and unnatu-ral crime' (that is, an act of gross indecency with another man) at the Gordon Coffee Tavern. Opened in 1880, the Gordon Coffee Tavern stood on the corner of Custom House Street and Bute Street in Cardiff and was owned by Edward Thomas (Cochfarf), one of the most prominent temperance campaigners in the city. In addition to the temperance cafe on the ground floor, there were several storeys of lodgings above which were often used by sailors and other itinerant workers, although it was never quite as sophisticated a part of 'queer commercial sociability' as the tearooms of New York or the coffee shops of London or the one run by Edward Carpenter and his friends in Sheffield.[3]

The pub, of course, was central to this homosocial world and navigated by those 'in the know' without affecting the wider social environment. As Rhys Davies explained to a friend in 1941,

> I discovered, after all, two 'sinks of iniquity' – a couple of 'gayish' pubs, rather low, where the local military and RAF foregathered for sing-songs etc, with a sprinkling of their good-hearted, apple-cheeked, if boisterous, wenches. I sang with them – folk songs, old ballads, hymns etc etc. I met an amusing RAF boy from Yorkshire, very camp. Also two bits of native nonsense.[4]

Such scenes were not limited to wartime; they might have been in evidence in any one of the pubs frequented by sailors in the docklands of Barry, Cardiff, Newport or Swansea. The Blue Anchor on St Mary's Street and the York Hotel on the East Wharf were typical. Indeed, the York Hotel had a stark reputation in the late nineteenth century as a place of violence, habitual drunkards, out of hours selling, and as a venue where prostitutes regularly plied for business, although it also claimed a certain respectability because of captains who popped in for a drink after visiting the neighbouring Custom House.[5] Nevertheless in 1887, the landlady, Sarah Ann Lewis, was cautioned for 'knowingly permitting her premises to be an habitual resort of women of ill-fame' and warned not to allow it to happen again.[6] She left the pub a few years later, just prior to major refurbishment and a clear attempt to clean up the hotel's image. In contrast to their reputation as places of solicitation, how and why either the York Hotel or the Blue Anchor became known as gay-friendly by the early 1970s is more difficult to establish.

Yet such spaces were central to gay socialisation throughout the twentieth century, and remained so in Newport, where they were often little more than parts of pubs or hotel bars, until the late 1980s. By then, the local press observed: 'even the jibes from young "straights" have abated now that the gay scene has become an accepted and common part of Newport's nightlife.'[7] Venues included the Waterloo Hotel, an Edwardian former docklands pub and, at times, brothel, which more than deserved its hardy reputation; the back bar of the Greyhound Inn on Cambrian Road; the Market Tavern on Griffin Street; the Crow's Nest and the Stage Door, both of which were on North Street; the King's Head, where some felt they had to 'act as if in Burton's front window'; the Speakeasy; and the Charleston and Cavern clubs. It was a similar situation in Barry at the lounge bars of the Barry Hotel and the Victoria Hotel, and in Merthyr Tydfil, where the Red Cow, Ye Olde Express and the Central Hotel provided the best opportunities in the Valleys, despite the observation by some travellers that the town had the 'most boring gay scene ever visited'![8] The Salisbury Hotel in Ferndale was the only other gay-friendly venue in the coalfield, and visitors could buy copies of *Gay News*.[9]

North Wales was no more exciting than the coalfield. In seaside resorts, hotel lounges such as the Rembrandt Bar at the Washington Hotel or the Orme Bar at the Alexandra Hotel, both in Llandudno, the Harp Inn in Caernarfon, the Blue Bell in Conwy, or the cellar bar at the Hotel Morville in Rhyl were the staple of 1970s gay nightlife. Students in Bangor congregated in the front bar of the King's Arms. The Drovers Arms in Howey on the outskirts of Llandrindod Wells was known as being particularly gay-friendly in the mid-1970s and promoted as such in newspapers and newsletters. Little changed in the 1980s except the names of the pubs and hotels which were gay-friendly: the Neville Hotel or the Viking Bar at the Imperial Hotel in Llandudno, the Westminster Hotel in Rhyl, the Walsh Arms Hotel in Llanddewi to the north of Llandrindod Wells, and the Belle Vue Royal Hotel in Aberystwyth (albeit strictly in term time). Although gay discos had been organised at the Orme Bar by CHE in 1980 and 1981, it was still possible in 1983 for a group of younger lesbians and gays to 'create the only gay bar ... in Anglesey and the North Wales Coast', which they ran for a short period at the student union in Bangor.[10] By 1985, though, Bangor GaySoc reported that

Many people regard North Wales as, socially speaking, 'the pits' for heterosexuals, the number of clubs being few, the distance between them great and the closing times down right ridiculous. So what, you may well ask, has North Wales to offer for Lesbians and Gay Men. The answer, obviously, can only be not very much. There is a bar for Lesbian and Gay people in Llandudno, named The Cavern which has a fairly large clientele. Then, just outside the border in Chester, there is a night club called Olivers which is very rarely anything but packed.[11]

The only other venue to open outside of Cardiff and Swansea was the Talk of the Abbey in Neath which ran quite successfully as a part-time gay space in 1983.[12] Located in the refurbished Windsor Cinema, it had originally opened in 1979 as a non-gay venue, but the proprietors recognised that they could increase trade on otherwise quiet nights of the week, such as Wednesdays and Sundays, by targeting a gay audience.[13] Given the limited opportunities available in south Wales, the Talk of the Abbey proved very popular, drawing patrons from Swansea and as far away as Chepstow and Bristol. But the club also drew the attention of more hostile campaigners, and in the autumn of 1983 a Labour councillor launched a campaign to have the club closed on the grounds that it was discriminating against non-homosexuals.[14] When magistrates discussed the club's licence a few months later, local police said that on one visit they had found 'one couple in a sensual embrace and another male couple were holding hands. A Lesbian couple were kissing and were also in a sensual embrace.' At least three male couples were also seen dancing.[15] With further lewd and homophobic evidence given to the licence hearing by police and residents, few were surprised that the club lost and was forced to close.[16]

The demise of the Talk of the Abbey forced Swansea revellers to rely once more on the limited but distinctive gay scene which had existed in the city since the early 1970s – Swansea was generally understood as being more accessible for women than elsewhere, and volunteers from Cardiff FRIEND often recommended that lesbians and bisexuals visit because there were 'a lot more women'. But there were also downsides: as one activist observed Swansea was 'pretty gay, but in a commercial bar way'. The first gay space was a cocktail bar at the Dolphin Hotel adjacent to the central market, although many found this 'very posh' and prone to 'clique forming'. There was a more agreeable atmosphere at the Grand Hotel, the Three Lamps Hotel, and at the George Hotel on the Mumbles.[17] From early 1973, the Cricketers near St Helen's cricket ground provided the clearest alternative even though, as one attendee put it, this was 'really a straight pub with gay overtones'. With its student vibe and gay-friendly atmosphere, it was packed at the weekends and there were 'a surprising number of gays there (more than at the Dolphin, our so-called gay pub)'.[18]

By the end of the 1970s, the Bush Hotel was the only advertised gay space in Swansea. The association was firmly denied by the local managers but accepted by the owners, Berni Inn, who explained to the *Western Mail* that 'we would not dream of having a 'no gays' policy. It is easy to over-dramatise this. We will not do anything about this listing. It is entirely up to *Gay News* what they publish.'[19]

The creation of Jingles (also known as the Palace) at the Palace Theatre on High Street and the nearby Champers transformed Swansea's gay nightlife in the 1980s. It was at Champers and the Palace that Nigel Owens first took the 'very positive step with regard to being honest about the fact that I was gay'. As he noted in his autobiography, *Half Time,*

Walking in on my own, with everyone seemingly staring at me, was a very strange and frightening experience. Not knowing what to do or say, I walked up to the bar and ordered a drink. Before long several people had come up to talk to me and most of them were very friendly. In fact I made some good friends that night ... I then moved on, with the few friends that I had made that night, to a gay nightclub just up the road called the Palace.[20]

The importance of the Palace and Champers, the fact that the former had initially opened as a members' club aside, was that they brought Swansea's gay scene out of the shadows of hotel bars, where the presence of gays and lesbians was contingent on the manager. For much of the twentieth century, Cardiff's gay scene was not all that different. Older working-class haunts, such as the Blue Anchor on St Mary's Street or the York Hotel on the east wharf of the canal, retained their importance as 'dens of deviance' and both the GLF and CHE met at the former in the early 1970s, as did the city's earliest lesbian campaign group. The Blue Anchor was also home to gay discos from at least the spring of 1972.[21] In the view of one contemporary observer, however,

The Cardiff Gay Scene is pathetic, and like all Gay scenes it is very hush-hush. One or two Gay Bars and that's it. And we don't like gay bars because they are little more than cattle markets: everyone knows you are there to pick someone up – but it's secret and shameful.[22]

The transformation of Cardiff's nightlife took place in the early 1960s. Nightclubs appeared for the first time, much to the disgust of older politicians such as S. O. Davies, who had previously

spoken vehemently in the House of Commons against late opening clubs in London. 'Babylon was a capital city once upon a
time', he said in 1949, 'and probably the licensing of its night
clubs contributed to its very unhappy ending ... I am satisfied that
there is no decent, human, or social necessity for this business.'
The Licensing committee in Cardiff was no less enthusiastic.[23]
Led by the Egyptian-born entrepreneur Annis Abraham, Cardiff
gained a series of glamorous venues from the mid-1960s.
Abraham came to prominence because of the success of his
Club Discs A'Gogo in Custom House Street, the Haven Club
in Butetown and the Sphinx Club in Leckwith Road, Canton.[24]
Opened in 1963 in the former Pavlova Dance Hall, the Sphinx
Club was richly decorated with hieroglyphics on the walls and
ancient Egyptian décor throughout. Its redevelopment had cost
£20,000. Then in 1966 Abraham opened his most ambitious
club yet: Cleopatra's on Custom House Street. Like the Sphinx
Club, it was lavishly themed with ancient Egyptian décor.[25] Later
that year he expanded the enterprise to Bristol and in 1968 he
opened Cleopatra's Palace in Caerleon Road, Newport.[26]

Annis Abraham's contribution to the development of a commercial gay scene in Cardiff was accidental, but nevertheless
important. During 1967, he began the process of converting the
upstairs area of the Cleopatra Club in Cardiff into a new venue.
Intended as a direct evocation of the theatreland clubs of London,
Abraham envisaged a 'chatty, rest-a-while type venture where
showbiz personalities can go in the extremely odd hours when
they are not working. A business connection is a qualification
of membership'.[27] Before it opened, Campbell Balfour, a Labour
councillor, complained that the club would provide a 'particularly
sleazy form of entertainment not in keeping with the cultural
buildings which surround it', but he could hardly have envisaged

what happened next.[28] The Showbiz Club opened that autumn.[29] It was not long before Abraham's new venture took on a different kind of atmosphere. In July 1968, the club was leased to Lenny Lancaster, whose flamboyance and homosexuality resulted in the Showbiz becoming Cardiff's first gay bar.[30] Writing in the *South Wales Echo* many years later, one former police officer remembered how the club 'attracted gay people of both sexes'.[31] The building was eventually destroyed by fire in 1977. As one newspaper put it at the time, 'The destruction of the Showbiz Club will deprive Cardiff homosexuals of what was one of their most popular meeting points.'[32]

But it was not, by then, the only gay bar in Cardiff. An early venue, recommended by volunteers at FRIEND to many first timers, was Roberts Bar at the Royal Hotel which was gay-friendly from the late-1960s, although managers were never that enthusiastic: 'it's a sign of the times', explained one of them in 1978, 'we shall not do anything about it even though we are not terribly in favour.'[33] The cellar bar at the nearby Grand Hotel was similarly accessible by the mid-1970s: it was here that all-gay discos were held in 1974 and 1975. The Bristol Hotel on Penarth Road, the Royal Oak on St Mary's Street, the Horse & Groom on Womanby Street, and the Castle Bar at the Angel Hotel variously provided gay-friendly spaces in this period as well. In his 1979 novel *Bob yn y Ddinas*, Siôn Eirian described this sort of venue in a scene which took place at the Duke of Wellington on a Sunday night some time in the late 1970s.

> I walk back, past the [Tabernacle] chapel again and into the small lounge of the Duke of Wellington ... I light a cigarette and stand in the corner near the bar. I don't know anyone here. Of course. Only Toni, the homosexual barman ... This

is a bar for people like Toni, you see. One of them is a busi-
nessman, in a smart suit n'all.

I remember one night when a middle-aged woman came
in, sat at the bar and started buying drinks for all and sundry
(everyone except me, of course). And then I noticed, it was
a man, in a skirt, heels, and a light brown wig ... He and the
boys were having a lot of fun, buying pints and telling jokes
and laughing.

... It's why Toni advises some customers to go to the other
lounge to be served. If a young couple, or a group of students,
or a husband and wife, come in accidentally, Toni explains
in a quiet voice that the bar has been hired by a group for
their meeting. Lies, of course, but it avoids embarrassment.

There was a clear sense of separation between gay and non-gay
patrons, either using back bars, separate lounges, or through
the careful intervention of the bar staff to maintain a distinction between the two. Yet nothing was underground or hidden
about bars of this kind: they were a place to which an individual could go if they were 'in the know', and could be stumbled
upon accidentally. Alternative music venues such as Club Roma
on Churchill Way, the New Moon on Mill Lane or Sam's Bar
on St Mary's Street (previously the Terminus), also appealed to
lesbian and gay revellers.

The first deliberately established gay club to open in Cardiff
was SIRS, a members-only venue situated above the Matisse
Bar on St Mary's Street, for which a key was required to enter –
although these were as anonymous and indistinct as those fitting
a standard Yale lock – and whose existence and location was kept
quiet. One Rhondda man trying out the scene for the first time
explained to a FRIEND volunteer in 1977 that he had failed to

find the club when he went looking on a night out. In the opinion of *Ar Dâf*, the magazine of the Welsh-language student union in Cardiff, the Matisse was a 'sexist place [because] it costs more for women to go in'. Women were only able to buy half pints, unlike the male customers (a rule which also existed at SIRS), and there was a total ban on jeans, which limited its appeal to younger people. Perhaps because of its neighbour's reputation, perhaps not, SIRS had an 'older male clientele', as one former visitor recalled, but it also had 'a tiny dance floor which was wired to flash on in random abandon. I thought this highly sophisticated.'[34] Following SIRS were clubs such as Hunters, which opened in the Oxford Arcade in 1978 and was owned by Lenny Lancaster, and the Tunnel Club.

In its heyday in the 1980s, the Tunnel was the premier late-night gay venue in Cardiff and drew crowds and performers from far and wide – those who went, went 'a lot'.[35] One of its most popular acts was Lily Savage. In his memoir, Paul O'Grady considered it 'one of my favourite venues'.[36] Barbara Windsor also appeared. Situated down an alleyway, the Tunnel was a long, meandering venue. On the inside revellers danced along to club beats, cheering on drag artists, taking poppers, or watching Mr Wet Y-Fronts competitions on the stage. Like SIRS, the Tunnel had a macho reputation (accompanied by a separate men-only bar) and was unsurprisingly regarded as the most masculine 'of the capital's gay nightspots'.[37] Paul Burston recalled that 'the only strangers at the Tunnel were those people who didn't have big moustaches and a City and Guilds in fan-dancing'. Yet for all its obviously popularity, the Tunnel club was never quite able to become the centre of gay life in Cardiff.

That role fell to the King's Cross. Behind its doors 'they were all there – gay men, art students, straight girls with necklaces made out of lovebites, dope heads, a smattering of lesbians, and goths.'[38] It was where UCC's GaySoc met each week for its social events.[39] Potential rivals included the Golden Cross which was regarded as being rougher, but no less fun; the Crown, which opened on Sunday afternoons when the King's Cross did not; and the Red Dragon Inn at Cardiff Central Station whose landlord, Peter Coff, was active in fundraising for AIDS charities in the late-1980s.[40] As John Williams put it, the Golden Cross was 'for prostitutes and people who just didn't care' – a reputation it had had since the nineteenth century. The Red Dragon on the other hand had customers who 'tended to be older ... the average age is between 25 and 40, and is not the usual – and I use the word advisedly – lager lout contingent'.[41] Somewhere in between was the Panorama, a 'gay pub with a mixed clientele' situated on the ground floor of an early 1970s office block on David Street. According to an understated profile in *Gair Rhydd* in 1986, it had a 'nice atmosphere'.

For those entering gay bars for the first time, there was an obvious sense of trepidation. One man from Merthyr, a bus driver, was taken to the King's Cross by a volunteer from Cardiff FRIEND in the early 1980s. He was nervous at first and had to be reassured that he would not meet anyone from Merthyr who would know him. The volunteer recorded in the log, 'oh dear – the rugby cup final was on and we met the Merthyr mob – he handled it very well and afterwards laughed as they did not know what pub they were in'. After Tim Foskett went to the Terminus for the first time as a fresher at Cardiff in October 1984, he wrote about the experience anonymously for the Free Word column of *Gair Rhydd*:

> With all my courage and some that I had borrowed, I walked
> into this rather dark foreboding pub. There were only a few

people in it – I'm sure they all heard my heart beating, I could see no obvious place to go. I doubt that I have ever been so scared, alone in an "alternative" if not specifically gay bar in a town I had lived in for a week. The barman was very helpful when I eventually managed to ask if he knew where the 'University group' was. I was shown into a nearly empty bar, with 6 or 7 people in – my heart was still having a wail of a time, but I calmed down during the evening.[42]

Reflecting more recently on his experiences, he noted that the relatively small size of the Cardiff scene made it more manageable as a newly out teenager: it was a 'good landing'.

A year or so after Foskett arrived, the *South Wales Echo* published an exposé on gay Cardiff. It noted the clear division between gay men and women and the tendency for 'pairs of short-haired, plain-dressed, serious-looking young ladies' to cuddle up in venues such as 'the small and sweaty' Radcliff's on Westgate Street – its upstairs neighbour, the Square Club, was popular with the alternative music crowd and the venue for the Manic Street Preachers' first gig in Cardiff. Other lesbian or women-only events were held in community centres such as the Star in Splott and leisure centres such as Channel View in Grangetown. The article was an important advert for the community – several rang in to FRIEND and remarked on having seen it – and clearly identified gay venues for the first time. This was itself a significant step forward. During the first pride march a few months earlier, organisers had fly-postered the city centre advertising a social event at the Tunnel Club, but the owners had 'gone berserk' and threatened to sue if a section of the poster advertising the club's location was not removed. In the dead of night, Foskett and others went back around the city tearing the bottom off the poster to preserve the club's anonymity a little while longer.[43]

Such anxiety was by no means overblown or unfounded. Although gay bashing incidents were less frequent than they had been in the 1960s, they had not entirely ceased. In a revealing interview published in *Gair Rhydd* just a few years before the pride march, one student had noted that there was a 'general anti-gay feeling in Cardiff', especially in the city centre where the National Front were active. He knew of 'several gays at the drama college who have been beaten up by thugs in town' and was conscious that 'if I went into the Dyfed bar on a Wednesday night and announced I was gay, I'd expect to be laid into'. Nevertheless, so long as one didn't draw attention to oneself, the student union bar was a 'comparatively "safe" [place] for gays to meet'.[44]

Today, a rainbow flag flying over a pub or a club is the quintessential symbol of gay liberation. But they are in decline: more than 50 per cent closed in London between 2007 and 2017 and all but a handful of venues in Cardiff have disappeared.[45] This may reflect changing social attitudes – the development of pubs and clubs marked a specific moment in the development of public gay culture – and is not unusual in countries, such as Denmark, Iceland and Norway, where homophobia and segregation have considerably declined. But it also reflects the steady dissolution of pubs and clubs more generally and the retreat of evening entertainment into the home. Decline has been more pronounced amongst gay venues because of the dominance of pubs and clubs; indeed, the challenge for the liberation movement was to develop alternatives for a range of social activities and to provide access to information. Bristol had a gay centre, Bath a weekly cafe, and London, Plymouth, Brighton and Edinburgh bookshops.

Such alternatives were always far more limited in Wales and have now almost entirely disappeared; Newport had its own cafe for a time in the 1970s, Cardiff and Swansea had street theatre groups, and gay centres and youth clubs were opened during the 1980s.[46] The strongest alternatives were the radical book-shops such as the 108 community bookshop in Cardiff, Focus and subsequently Neges in Swansea (the latter had its origins in the women's liberation movement) and the Quarry bookshop at the Centre for Alternative Technology in Machynlleth. They provided access to lesbian and gay literature and newspapers and magazines, as did campus shops and newsagents that stocked *Gay News* or the *Pink Paper*. The mail order services of Gay's the Word in London were similarly essential to the provision of infor-mation, pamphlets, newsletters and a full range of fiction and non-fiction aimed at lesbian and gay audiences in areas where there was no other alternative or access was limited.[47] Women's centres in Bangor, Cardiff and Swansea, and the Rights and Information Bureau in Cardiff also functioned as advice bureaux.

In his 2010 play *Llwyth* (Tribe), Dafydd James captured the essence of the contemporary gay scene in Cardiff's most familiar venues, the King's Cross and Club X. This was a culture (not always at ease with itself) given over to alcohol, drugs and the morning after the night before full of discarded polystyrene chip cartons and vomit, but absent the political underpinnings of the liberation movement of the 1970s and the HIV/AIDS activism of the 1980s.[48] Carefully woven into the play are questions of iden-tity, a desire to present a more positive version of homosexuality amongst Welsh-speakers, a direct challenge to notions of mascu-linity and heteronormative historical traditions. But liberation in the political sense? Thus *Llwyth* captured the visible and public queer community of the early twenty-first century: a community which could dance the night away in a small number of venues without ever concerning itself, as earlier generations did, with changing the world.

Notes

1. James Nott, *Going to the Palais: A Social and Culture History of Dancing and Dance Halls in Britain, 1918–1960* (Oxford, 2015), p. 240.
2. John Williams, *Bloody Valentine: A Killing in Cardiff* (London, 1995), p. 88.
3. Houlbrook, *Queer London*, p. 88; George Chauncey, *Gay New York: Gender, Urban Culture and the Making of the Gay Male World, 1890–1940* (New York, 1994).
4. NLW MS 23106 E 13, cited in Osborne, *Rhys Davies*, pp. 93–4.
5. *SWDN*, 22 October 1872, 14 October 1886; *WM*, 9 April 1891.
6. *Weekly Mail*, 21 May 1887.
7. *SWA*, 21 January 1988.
8. *Spartacus International Gay Guide* (1980), p. 579; *GN* 42 (14 March 1974).
9. *GN*, 48 (6 June 1974).
10. *Gay Noise*, 8 (20 November 1980); *Gay Noise*, 12 (29 January 1981); *GN*, 262 (13 April 1983).
11. *Seren*, 14 October 1985.
12. Although CHE had met at the Castle Hotel in Neath in the 1970s. *GN*, 85 (1975).
13. *The Stage*, 24 May 1979, 3 November 1983, 15 March 1984; *SWEP*, 22 October, 31 October 1983.
14. *SWEP*, 19 October 1983.
15. *SWEP*, 28 February 1984.
16. *The Stage & Television Today*, 15 March 1984.
17. *GN*, 38 (17 January 1974).
18. Leeds Gay Liberation, *Broadsheet*, 14 (February 1973).
19. *WM*, 24 August 1978.
20. Nigel Owens, *Half Time* (Talybont, 2009).
21. Leeds Gay Liberation, *Broadsheet*, 4 (February 1972).
22. Adrian Birch, 'It doesn't pay to be gay ... YET!!', *Broadsheet* (Cardiff), 21 October 1971.
23. *The Stage*, 26 March 1964.
24. *The Stage*, 30 January, 29 October 1964, 12 October 1967. Discs A'Gogo was named after the music programme on Television Wales and West (TWW)

of the same name. Jamie Medhurst, *A History of Independent Television in Wales* (Cardiff, 2010), p. 69.

25. *The Stage*, 3 February 1966.

26. *The Stage Year Book*, 36 (1967), 329; *The Stage*, 19 May, 9 June, 21 December 1966. The Cardiff club was sold to Abraham's great rival Gino Rabaiotti in 1968. *The Stage*, 1 February 1968.

27. *The Stage*, 28 September 1967.

28. *The Stage*, 16 March 1967.

29. *The Stage*, 12 October 1967.

30. GA, DSWP/20/3 – Cardiff Licensing Register, Clubs, S9: Showbiz Club.

31. *SWE*, 4 April 2013.

32. *The Cardiff Link*, 9 (19 January 1978).

33. *WM*, 24 August 1978.

34. Steven Lewis-Jones, 'Comment', *https://davidsmemoirs.wordpress.com/2016/12/28/tales-of-the-coleherne/* (accessed, 24 November 2017).

35. Tim Foskett interview.

36. Paul O'Grady, *Still Standing: My Savage Years* (London, 2012), p. 286.

37. *SWE*, 20 November 1985; *GR*, 14 October 1986.

38. Paul Burston, *Queen's Country* (London, 2008).

39. Tim Foskett interview; although for some of 1984–5, GaySoc met at the Terminus instead. *GR*, 23 January 1985.

40. *The Stage*, 19 May 1988.

41. *The Stage*, 24 January 1991.

42. *GR*, 24 October 1984.

43. Tim Foskett interview.

44. *GR*, 19 November 1980

45. *https://www.london.gov.uk/press-releases/mayoral/mayor-pledges-support-to-lgbt-venues-in-london* 'Accessed 5 July 2018'.

46. *GN*, 85 (October 1975); Leeds Gay Liberation, *Broadsheet*, 23 (February–March 1974); *GN*, 44 (11 April 1974).

47. Tim Foskett interview; Richard Coles, *Fathomless Riches: Or How I Went from Pop to Pulpit* (London, 2014); *Gay Noise*, 3 (11 September 1980); *Gay Noise*, 4 (25 September 1980); *Gay Noise*, 7 (6 November 1980). The Gay's the Word *Newsletter* and *Review* published from 1980 onwards provide a clear indication of the material made available by the bookshop.

48. Dafydd James, *Llwyth* (Aberystwyth, 2010); Dafydd James, 'Y Queer Yn Erbyn Y Byd', *Taliesin*, 151 (2014).

PART III

Changing The World

CHAPTER FIVE

Law Reform and Afterwards

W*ill Vice Go Underground?* asked the *Western Mail* on
5 September 1957.[1] The front-page headline was the
paper's response to the publication, the previous day, of Sir John
Wolfenden's report into homosexual offences and prostitution.
'The liveliest moral controversy for years is likely to be sparked
off by the recommendations', the paper remarked; 'it is sure to
be attacked by many for being too lenient and "progressive,"
and by others for being too harsh.' In fact, the series of *vox pops*
which appeared in the *Western Mail* over the next few months
pointed to a society more aligned with the recommendations
than against them, albeit for different reasons. The city's stipen-
diary magistrate, Guy Sixsmith, observed that 'the committee's
recommendations are sound and reasonable'. Magistrates were
perhaps motivated by contemporary conditions: cruising and
cottaging in counterpoint with a steady stream of violence. By the
1960s magistrates were regularly told that 'queer bashing' had
become something of a 'sport'.[2] It was also the case in Swansea.[3]

A more conservative legal response to the Wolfenden
Report was put forward by senior police officers, including the
Chief Constable of Glamorgan, Cecil Haydn Watkins. Called

to give evidence on behalf of the Association of Chief Police Officers, Watkins was one of the few Welsh voices heard by the Wolfenden Committee. He iterated the collective view of Chief Constables that the law should remain unchanged and pointed out that this was a vice created in London which little troubled the provinces.[4] The stance was shared by the then Director of Public Prosecutions, Sir Theobald Mathew, and his successor Sir Norman Skelhorn.[5] Chief constables were clearly irritated by the report's eventual recommendations, particularly the suggestion that the existing law was not working. But that was true. Of the more than 6,000 homosexual offences reported to the police in 1956, only a third were proceeded with. It was a similar figure in 1957.[6]

Beyond the magistracy and the police, the report was regarded as an opportunity to reorient public understanding. The rector of St Fagans thought that Wolfenden was 'on a pretty sound wicket' and explained his belief in homosexuality as 'the third sex' – an indication of a spectrum of attraction rather than the perceived wisdom of deviance.[7] The Swansea-born Jewish poet and teacher Mimi Josephson took this further, arguing: 'surely no-one can believe that a man deserves a prison sentence because he is born with homosexual tendencies, any more than he does because of being born blind or with a club foot.' She continued, 'it is certainly time for drastic changes both in the law ... and in our attitude ... There should be neither legal nor moral condemnation of men who are guilty neither of sin nor of crime.'[8]

Wider polling conducted in the wake of the Wolfenden Report showed that a significant proportion of the public were indeed in favour of implementing its recommendations. The *Daily Mirror* noted that of the more than 11,000 people it asked, around 5,500 were supportive, with just over 6,000 against.[9] In Wales, as in England, those living in southern counties were more likely to be in favour than those living in northern areas. Similar results were evident in a Gallup poll for the *News Chronicle*: 38 per cent were in favour, 47 per cent were not. The remainder did not know. Reporting on both, the *Guardian* noted: 'one would hardly have been surprised if so novel a proposal, about an act so repulsive to most people, had set off an emotional explosion, with ten or twenty to one repudiating the recommendation.'[10] That was not the case.

Although Welsh society was not yet 'permissive', a substantial number clearly felt that prohibition was not working. Proponents of reform in the 1950s often urged the reclassification of homosexuality as a medical 'disorder' or 'condition' rather than a form of criminal behaviour. Speaking to a meeting of the Cardiff Fabian Society in June 1958, Eirene White, the Labour MP for East Flintshire, a proponent of legal reform, indicatively put forward the medical case. She said: 'the fact that it [homosexuality] is now regarded as a criminal offence must surely lead to fear and blackmail ... once the fear of blackmail or the fear of losing a job was gone many homosexuals would seek treatment.'[11] But treatment for what, exactly? One Swansea doctor explained the prevailing view: 'as yet, we know little about the cause and nature of this condition. In many cases there is evidence to suppose that it is a psychological state, due to relational maladjustments affecting the subject in the early years of childhood.'[12]

The legal reform movement within Parliament, in which Welsh MPs took a leading role, thus navigated the tensions between a conservative position, which held to criminality and sin, and a 'progressive' medicalisation of homosexuality, which supported 'treatment', 'self-control' and integration – if only the negative conditions were removed. The extra-Parliamentary reform movement, known as the Homosexual Law Reform Society, was launched in May 1958. It followed the publication in *The Times* of a letter in support of Wolfenden signed by dozens of prominent political and cultural figures including former prime minister Clement Attlee, philosopher Bertrand Russell and the Labour MP for Pembrokeshire, Desmond Donnelly. The signatories were gathered by Tony Dyson, a lecturer in the English Literature department at UCNW, Bangor, who wrote to them initially on notepaper headed with the college address.[13] The Homosexual Law Reform Society had limited presence in Wales, however. Neither its formation nor its first major public meetings in 1960 were reported by the Welsh press, although readers of national newspapers such as the *Daily Herald* were kept informed.[14]

In the absence of widespread activity in favour of reform, the involvement of Welsh MPs in the Parliamentary movement can seem, in retrospect, unexpected, perhaps even a 'niche issue'. This ignores a clear trend, however. Desmond Donnelly, the first Welsh MP to seek change, had called for a royal commission on homosexual law reform in 1954, pointing to 'public disquiet over police methods' as the motivating factor.[15] He later described the pre-1967 law as a 'blackmailer's charter'.[16] But Donnelly was not alone in accepting the need for change. When Kenneth Robinson's motion calling for decriminalisation was moved in June 1960, it was supported by a cross-party group of MPs which included Roy Jenkins, Jeremy Thorpe and Margaret Thatcher. Heavily defeated by two hundred and thirteen votes to ninety nine, the division revealed, for the first time, the spectrum of opinion amongst Welsh MPs. Six voted in favour, a higher proportion than amongst Scottish or English

MPs, and eight voted against; the remainder abstained or were absent.

All those voting for the motion came from the Labour benches: Leo Abse (Pontypool), Elfed Davies (Rhondda East), Desmond Donnelly (Pembrokeshire), Walter Padley (Ogmore), George Thomas (Cardiff West), and Eirene White (Flintshire East). Three Labour MPs from the coalfield voted against the measure, alongside five Conservative MPs – an indication, perhaps, of a strand of social conservatism several historians have identified in post-war Welsh society.[17] They were S. O. Davies (Merthyr), Ness Edwards (Caerphilly), and Arthur Probert (Aberdare). Their votes were counterbalanced by Welsh-born Labour MPs representing English and Scottish seats, such as Emrys Hughes (South Ayrshire) and Hilary Marquand (Middlesbrough East) who voted in favour.[18] The absentees included both Liberal MPs, Clement Davies and Roderick Bowen. Of the Labour MPs absent, some such as Llywelyn Williams, the Abertillery MP, were undoubtedly in favour of reform and had set out their reasoning in previous debates; the opinions of others were not known.[19]

It is clear from their public statements that reformers were not 'allies' in the twenty-first-century sense. Eirene White told her Parliamentary colleagues: 'I regard homosexual behaviour as something extremely repugnant.' Leo Abse used similar terms. Rather, these were individuals who represented a strand within the Labour Party committed to fairness within the legal system and to tolerance – their central concern was privacy not an expression of moral approval.[20] This was apparent in Llywelyn Williams's contribution to the Commons Wolfenden debate in 1958. Amidst emotionally-charged proceedings full of the rhetoric of sin and danger, equality and fairness, Williams took to his feet just as the clock struck ten in the evening. He said:

We should be as free from emotionalism as possible in our analysis of these problems and difficulties. I admit that it is not easy for the so-called normal person, such as myself, whose physical and sexual life is happily integrated into a satisfactory marital relationship, to be unemotional or object-ive in these matters. I confess that it is only on the basis of knowledge acquired by extensive reading on the subject plus a deliberate act of sympathetic imagination that enables me to understand or even try to understand the problems and difficulties of a homosexual. But the effort must be made, otherwise there can be no progress in dealing with this admittedly difficult problem.

He stressed the need for further understanding 'into the cause and origin of homosexual behaviour', indicative of the medical-ised perspective used by reformers, and thanked the Wolfenden Committee for drawing attention to the criminalisation of homo-sexual 'offences' compared with the legal sanction of adultery. Williams concluded:

While society could never give moral approval to that type of behaviour, since it takes place in the privacy of a house-hold, it should not rank as a criminal offence any more than heterosexual behaviour between consenting adults in pri-vate, such as adultery and fornication, to which again society could never give moral approval, should rank as a criminal offence ... We who legislate in this House should not be too timorous in supporting these recommendations because public opinion may be lagging behind. In a sense, we are the creators of public opinion. Certainly, someone must give a lead in these matters. The Wolfenden Committee has done its job splendidly in this regard by presenting us with this great social document. We should do our part in revealing a similar sanity, understanding and determination in implementing the Report.[21]

A similar stance was taken by Leo Abse. He spoke on radio and television consistently setting out the case for separating legal fairness and moral toleration. Changing the law, as he explained in a discussion broadcast on the BBC Home Service in June 1962, would bring Britain into line with the majority of Western Europe. 'No one suggests that France and Italy and Spain and the Netherlands and Norway and Sweden and Denmark are all going to rack and ruin and are full of sin', he remarked, 'because the law is more permissive there'. Abse continued, addressing the Conservative MP, Edward Gardner,

> Your government will shortly, it hopes ... take us into the Common Market, it will be a curiosity of status, will it not, if a man can be living with an adult let us say in Denmark, and if he comes into this country, he can find himself subjected to the original law? The point I'm making is that these other countries have not found that homosexuality spread and became rife, although in fact they have different laws, in some cases more permissive laws for hundreds of years. And I do not believe that this country is more full of sin and immorality than other countries.[22]

Abse's argument changed little in the five years it took thereafter to bring about reform, which was eventually passed by Parliament in July 1967.

The Sexual Offences Act introduced into the law a strict definition of privacy. For sex to be legal it had to between two men aged over twenty one, but it could not take place in a room where more than two people were present or in a lavatory which could be accessed by the public. In effect, all doors and windows had to be locked, curtains closed, and lights out. Further caveats precluding legality included the 'commission' of sex – picking someone up in a bar, for instance, or telephoning or writing to make arrangements to meet. The limitations imposed by the 1967 act placed privacy and thus legality out of the reach of many, especially in overcrowded urban centres. In Cardiff, more than 6,000 people lived in cramped conditions, with almost 500 three-storey houses in the city classed as houses of multiple occupation. An average of more than six people lived in each of them.[23] The published figures were only those known to the city's housing officers and were an underestimate – indeed the figure grew to more than 1,000 houses of multiple occupation by 1972.[24] For those without privacy, law reform offered little comfort.

The flaws in the Sexual Offences Act, obvious as much then as in retrospect, encouraged campaigners to demand further, and wider-ranging, legislation to remove the threat of arrest and criminal prosecution entirely. Experiences and methods were similar to those adopted by the women's movement, the black civil rights campaign, the student movement, the peace movement and green activism, and there was to be a good deal of cross-over between them, especially in Cardiff and Swansea. The gay movement had two major components: the radical Gay Liberation Front which took inspiration from the United States and those forms of activism apparent there in the aftermath of the Stonewall riots of 1969; and the Campaign for Homosexual

Equality, which pursued legislative reforms such as equalisation of the age of consent, the provision of sex education in schools, legal protection in the workplace and freedom from discrimination in housing and healthcare. Typically, the Gay Liberation Front, which formed at the LSE in October 1970, has been regarded as the more militant organisation, with the Campaign for Homosexual Equality understood to be more moderate, although the distinction was misleading and the boundary between the two was porous. The GLF's activities tended to be concentrated in university towns, whereas CHE was more widespread.

CHE emerged out of the North-Western Committee for Homosexual Law Reform, which was founded in October 1964 by Allan Horsfall and Colin Harvey, two Manchester-based members of the Homosexual Law Reform Society.[25] The branch was renamed the Committee for Homosexual Equality in 1969 becoming the Campaign for Homosexual Equality in 1971.[26] Harvey was a social worker working for the Church of England's North-West Board of Social Responsibility and arranged, through the bishop of Middleton, Ted Wickham, for church premises in Manchester to be used for the committee's meetings. Harvey was also involved in the establishment of the Scottish gay rights organisation, the Scottish Minorities Group, in 1969, although he was not himself gay. Horsfall, on the other hand, was. He worked for the National Coal Board and served as a Labour councillor in Nelson, Lancashire, by which means he effectively pioneered the links between the Labour Party and gay rights.[27] Horsfall regarded the campaign for homosexual equality as a left-wing issue strongly linked to social class.

In many respects, Horsfall's experiences in the north of England mirrored those of Ray Davies (1930–2015) who faced considerable challenges trying to convince the Labour Party and his NUM lodge to engage with gay rights.[28] As he recalled, 'I tried to bring it up in the lodge ... no they didn't want to do with it. We've got to struggle to earn our money and to get better conditions, that's a sideline. I tried every way I could to do it. I went to see the MP, we done everything.' Davies was motivated to act after speaking to a fellow miner who had been ostracised by colleagues for his homosexuality. Whilst on national service at the end of the 1940s, Davies received a letter from his father telling him that his friend had committed suicide because of the social persecution. Davies continued:

> And from that day on, I tell you, I became an avid cam-
> paigner against homophobia. When I joined the Labour
> Party [in 1958], I went to a Labour Party conference, I went
> to see MPs who I knew were sympathetic. We agreed to put
> a fringe meeting on and three people turned up. The MPs
> said oh well we'll leave it. No, I said, we bloody won't leave
> it. If it's only three people, we will do the meeting, I said,
> and we will make a report and we will circulate to every
> member of bloody Parliament to know about the injustice
> that has been going on a section of our community. So the
> meeting went ahead and we got the report out and the next
> year we had twenty at the meeting. The year after that we
> had fifty.[29]

The fringe meetings to which Davies referred were part of the steady emergence of gay rights activism within the Labour Party, culminating in the formation of the Gay Labour Group in 1975.[30] Many of those involved in establishing the GLG were CHE members; they organised fringe meetings at Labour's annual

conference and gay discos, and encouraged members to push
their constituency parties to propose motions supportive of gay
rights and to affiliate to the Gay Labour Group. In 1978, the
group was renamed the Labour Campaign for Gay Rights. It
adopted the more inclusive name Labour Campaign for Lesbian
and Gay Rights in 1982, and today is known as LGBT Labour.
LCLGR remained a relatively small pressure group: 200 members had joined by 1983 and there were ten directly affiliated
CLPs, although most of them were in London – with meetings
often held at Gay's the Word bookshop. In Wales, activists in
Swansea and Llanelli were the only ones to have a discernible
relationship with LCLGR in the early 1980s.[31]

Labour were not alone in developing a gay rights platform
in the 1970s and 1980s, of course, although they were the largest political party to do so. The Communist Party were the
first to embrace gay rights, doing so in 1976.[32] Plaid Cymru
debated the subject for the first time at their national conference in Swansea in 1978 as part of a composite motion on race
and minorities. As initially presented, however, gay rights were
absent, and the purpose of the debate was simply a renewal of the
party's 'total opposition to all prejudice on the grounds of race,
creed or language'. Following an intervention from the Cardiff
North-West constituency party, the motion was altered to include
'sexual preference'. Acceptance was not guaranteed, since the
same conference saw opposition to abortion rights expressed
by party members from Anglesey, Flintshire and Aberystwyth.
Nevertheless, by 1983 Plaid Cymru declared that it wished to
create 'a fair and equitable society in which all people living in
Wales, both women and men, should enjoy equal rights and equal
opportunities. We oppose discrimination on any grounds.'[33] A
similar stance was taken by the party's youth section.[34]

Yet in comparison with Labour and the Communist Party, active discussion about lesbian and gay rights within the nationalist movement was limited, with hardly any mention in the newsletters produced by constituencies and branches (even in Cardiff) or the party's national newspapers and magazines. No surprise that, in the late 1980s, Mike Parker recalled being 'invited to address a party conference on the subject of lesbian and gay rights for ... no card-carrying Plaidwyr were prepared to edge out of the closet far enough to the do the job themselves'.[35] Nor were Plaid Cymru particularly well connected to the gay rights movement as a whole: CHE and GLF were active within Labour circles but do not seem to have worked a great deal with the nationalists, even in areas where the latter was politically strong. Only occasionally did CHE in Gwynedd seek the support of the local MP, Dafydd Wigley. Whereas Plaid Cymru were supportive of gay rights, as evidenced by the voting record of its Members of Parliament, the party was also content to leave them in the background.[36]

The relationship between Labour and CHE reflected both a national trend – this was the case across Britain – and the concentration of the gay rights movement in Glamorgan and Monmouthshire where Labour was strongest. The first Welsh branch of CHE was formed as Cardiff–Newport early in 1972 by a pioneering group of nine. Most lived in Cardiff, but others travelled to the branch meetings at the Blue Anchor on St Mary's Street from communities as varied as Aberaman, Barry, Newport and Ystrad Mynach.[37] In the summer of 1972, the branch moved to the fledgling Chapter Arts Centre in Canton, and the more genial environment enabled a rapid expansion in the number of members. By November 1972, Cardiff–Newport CHE had over fifty members, ranging from students to pensioners.[38]

The branch convenor, Chris Johnson, an educational psychologist from Newport, explained the move away from the Blue Anchor in a letter to CHE's national organisers: 'although expensive (£2 per night) [it] has a bar which we can use at any time, theatre and cinema facilities and has the potential of becoming a really good centre for our membership with the added advantage of integration with their "straight" clientele.' The range of social activities made possible by Chapter almost certainly encouraged the growth of the gay rights movement in Cardiff and, with an increased membership, the branch was able to work alongside student support services, social services and general practitioners to improve the situation for the city's lesbian and gay population. CHE stickers were 'consistently turning up in the most unlikely places – even in library books and hymn books in churches!' One of those who joined was 'Fred', who explained in an interview with Jeffrey Weeks and Kevin Porter: 'I was nervous to a point when I first went in. I was coming up to eighty years old! And, of course, I've become one of the old contemptibles, one of the regulars aye.'[39] Fred's experience was unusual, but illustrated the intergenerational value of CHE, particularly for men.

CHE's appeal, even in Cardiff, was weaker amongst women. They tended to find the atmosphere overly masculine and attuned to the concerns of gay men.[40] Writing in *Gay News* in November 1972, Daphne Higuera, who lived Caerphilly, reflected honestly on the difficulties facing women in the burgeoning gay movement:

> Women do tend to remain in the background, a lot more than our brothers, there are many reasons for this. In the provinces, clubs are few and far between, and many of us don't care for group activities. In fact, I feel there are still many

who do not know these groups exist. I myself, until recently, didn't know CHE or Gay Lib existed, until I heard Speakeasy on the radio (GN1). There's one exception, of course, some knew they were gay very early, but not all of us realised we were gay until we were married with children, then what could we do? A divorce perhaps. That's not always easy when children are involved. And, admit it, who wants to know you when you've got ties? Do we have to wait maybe years, before we can start to live, too? Or will someone, somewhere, realise our need, too, and give us a chance to meet discreetly, not in clubs or bars, but with others like us who need to be discreet. Women have their cross to bear, too.[41]

The result of Daphne Higuera's intervention was the creation of a separate women's group, which began meeting at the Blue Anchor early in 1973.[42] In the words of Chris Johnson, the gay women's group was the 'only way we can get an appreciable number of women recruited'.[43] The South Glamorgan Gay Women's Group, based in Barry, followed by 1975. In the north, a women's group was not established until 1977 in part because although women were a clear minority in CHE Gwynedd, they nevertheless were a substantial minority comprising a third of branch members.[44] Separate organisation ultimately pre-figured the migration of many lesbian and bisexual women into the women's liberation movement over the course of the 1970s. In that setting, writes Deirdre Beddoe, 'lesbian women in Wales felt comfortable in "coming out" … the WLM enabled them to become visible'.[45] Although generally true, it was not always the case that women's liberation was free of prejudice. A strongly-worded debate occurred in the pages of the Cardiff women's liberation magazine in 1981 about heterosexism and the relationship between the liberation of women and the liberation of lesbian women, with lesbians accused of being (or assumed to be) 'man haters'.[46]

For a period at the start of the 1970s, Cardiff also had a branch of the Gay Liberation Front. Formed in July 1971, GLF members established the relationship between the gay movement and the Blue Anchor, held joint meetings with the women's liberation movement, and encouraged the Labour Party (especially student members in Cardiff and Swansea) to pay closer attention to gay rights. They circulated schools to encourage awareness and lobbied the city's librarian to place gay literature on open shelves rather than hiding it away in back offices and store cupboards.[47] One of those who joined the Cardiff GLF early on was Adrian Birch, a student at University College Cardiff who manned the stall at the 1971 Freshers' Fayre at which the GLF made its first appearance. He described the scene in the student newspaper:

> There, ill-equipped at less than 24 hours' notice, we were met with an almost unrelieved blaze of apathy. We gave out information printed by the RIB on happenings in Cardiff, legal rights, etc., to anyone who was not scared off by posters that declared "homosexuals demand the right to love". Nobody, it appeared, wanted to be associated with us. But we had one recruit direct, several sympathetic recruits oblique, and several who circulated the stand several times and, hopefully, memorised our address.[48]

Following Fresher's Fayre, Cardiff GLF organised leaflet drops, a series of talks in Cardiff and Swansea and a march against unemployment complete with traditional marching banner – the first gay march anywhere in Wales.[49]

Cardiff GLF had a particularly strong relationship with the Rights and Information Bureau situated at 58 Charles Street. Opened in December 1970, the RIB was modelled on BIT, the information centre founded in 1968 in Ladbroke Grove, London, by the journalist and photographer Hoppy Hopkins. Together with the 108 Bookshop on Salisbury Road, which opened in 1974, it provided access to a wide range of underground magazines and newspapers including the *Cardiff People's Paper* and the *International Times* and acted as a social space for people who couldn't go to the establishment, to the council offices'.[50] One volunteer, a young American, who worked at the centre in 1971, reflected:

> Basically people walked in off the street, or sometimes had heard of RIB, and we tried to help them by putting them in touch with any needed resource we could find. Or sometimes they just came in to sit for a while and have some soup or keep warm. RIB also received phone calls asking for information or assistance as well. There was one paid [member of] staff and she organised the agency and the volunteers. Money to sustain the agency was raised through jumble sales and concerts. There was a front room and a back room and a tiny bathroom on the second floor.[51]

Cardiff GLF fell into abeyance in September 1972, just as the CHE branch was beginning to grow, and underwent a series of identity changes (as Gay Liberation Cardiff and then as Canopy) before eventually folding by the mid-1970s. Most members joined CHE.

There was a similar experience in Swansea. Although Cardiff GLF had initially sought to establish a sister branch at the end of 1971, the attempt was met 'with an overwhelming roar of apathy' and the branch did not coalesce until the spring of 1972. Based at the university, it did not retain the GLF identity for very long either, recognising that in Swansea 'the "political" approach of the GLF was preventing more moderate gays coming forward'. They aligned with CHE and took the title GaySoc. According to one observer, 'the gay students, it appears, are quite prepared to live an isolated existence during their three years.'[52] The situation in Aberystwyth and Bangor was worse. The Aberystwyth GLF had a handful of members, three 'lesbians and one and a half men'; the convenor despaired: 'I do think a year's long enough to register that people don't want to know.'[53] As the Bangor convenor, Simon del Novo, noted knowingly, 'Our sympathies to Aber GLF – we know what you're up against.'[54] Perhaps the most unlikely branch was set up by two lesbians in Aberdare early in 1973 as the Heads of the Valleys GLF. Most of its activities were focused on social events at the Red Cow in Merthyr Tydfil.[55]

Throughout this period, gay rights activism together with efforts at forging a more public gay culture were conducted principally at the local level, with CHE branches in Cardiff and Newport working alongside those in Bristol and Bath as part of a regional network. There was little demand for an all-Wales gay movement, except within the student movement where the University of Wales and the National Union of Students provided a natural foundation. The first all-Wales gay rights conference was thus hosted by UCNW GaySoc in Bangor in November 1974, some eighteen months after the NUS had agreed to support the aims of the GLF at their Easter Conference in Exeter in 1973. The Bangor conference was spearheaded by the then president of UCNW student union, Ann Beynon. She was also the NUS

Wales executive member responsible for the gay rights campaign. Linked to CHE, the conference enjoyed a modest amount
of media coverage including interviews with participants on the
BBC's 'Good Morning Wales'. Although there was a determination to unite the various factions of the gay movement in Wales
into one body, this was never achieved except through the activities of the university GaySocs. During the 1980s, as Tim Foskett
recalled, student lesbian and gay conferences on the various college campuses across Wales were a unique hive of activity but
stopped short of a pan-Wales movement.[56] Only with the establishment of Stonewall Cymru in 2003 did such an organisation
come into being.[57]

But what sort of activities did each of these organisations
engage in? They understood their role to be both political and
social, challenging the roots of oppression and providing information and support. Branches produced newsletters, held
conferences, discussed a variety of gay issues (admittedly pri-
marily relating to gay men) and organised social events and trips
– travel was a common feature of organised gay social life for
much of the 1970s and 1980s.[58] CHE Cardiff held weekly meetings in local venues such as Chapter Arts Centre, Club Roma and
the Blue Anchor but also travelled to the Moulin Rouge in Bristol
and to other gay venues further afield in Bath, Chippenham and
Cheltenham. CHE Newport held its fortnightly meetings at the
Civic Centre, social gatherings at the Waterloo Hotel and the
Charleston, and travelled to the Valentine's Club in Bath and to
the historic Nightingale Club in Birmingham. Of value to both
branches, especially on trips across the Severn Bridge, was a strip
club at Severn Beach, located not far from the motorway services.
As one Bristolian recalled of a night out at the Moulin Rouge,
there was 'a coach load of coal miners arriving from South Wales

in drag! After the club shut for the night many of us followed the coach to the Severn Bridge Service Area where the miners, still in drag, caused a sensation!'

The ability of gay rights organisations to act as pressure groups to bring about political change depended significantly on their relationship not with the commercial gay scene or with the university but with institutions of local government and the state, notably the police, health service, education committees and the probation service. Perhaps the most successful branch in this respect was CHE Newport. Formed in February 1973, the branch worked closely with the Labour-controlled borough council, who provided meeting space in the Civic Centre. This relationship with the council encouraged a certain boldness: CHE Newport pushed for the availability of information for gay youth in schools and asked direct questions about local policy on employing gay and lesbian teachers. Despite outrage from some members of the education committee, mostly from the Conservative Party, who demanded homosexual teachers be sacked immediately and any relationship with CHE avoided, there were progressive voices. These included the committee chair, and future mayor of the town, the Revd Cyril Summers who added that 'if sex education is properly given, then information on the subject of homosexuality should be included', and Paul Flynn, subsequently Labour MP for Newport West, who remarked

> I am sure we must be employing homosexual teachers now, just as we must be employing homosexual bus drivers and steelworkers. The suggestion that we should discriminate against them in this way is quite outrageous and scrapping the meeting would be an act of gross intolerance and unworthy of this council.

In the event, however, local government reform overtook these initiatives. The formation of Gwent County Council in 1974 changed the political complexion of the area and CHE Newport found it more difficult to press their case. In 1977, the local education authority refused to sanction distribution of CHE leaflets in schools after a four-year campaign.

As well as seeking the support of councillors, CHE Newport reached out to local Members of Parliament. Their findings provide valuable insights into the way in which the Labour Party in Monmouthshire responded to the campaign for gay rights. Leo Abse, the Pontypool MP, had steered the 1967 Sexual Offences Act through Parliament with support from the Ebbw Vale MP, Michael Foot, but during the 1970s Abse was vocal in his opposition to support for transgender men and women. In a television debate chaired by Robin Day and prompted by Jan Morris's gender reassignment surgery, Abse questioned the possibility that Morris was in fact a woman, declaring, in effect, 'just because you've had it chopped off, that doesn't make you a woman.' He pushed this view further in his review of Morris's memoir, *Conundrum*, published in the *Spectator* in April 1974. The book, he wrote,

> is essentially proselytising and, as such, in my judgement, immoral. It is one matter to insist that, with contemporary psychiatry helpless in the face of adult transsexualism, the law must afford as much protection as possible. [...] But it is another matter to label a pathological condition, albeit one that may have beneficial creative side effects, as magical or miraculous as Morris does.

Elsewhere in the review, Abse asserted his belief in the inherent bisexuality of humans – he regarded bisexuality as the default

setting – but refused to accept what he perceived to be the asser-
tion of 'superiority' by 'certain homosexuals' and 'transsexuals'
over 'mere heterosexuals'. As he had lamented in 1969, gays
and lesbians were failing to integrate into society preferring to
maintain a division instead, a division that Abse felt was entirely
artificial. He was not interviewed by Newport CHE.

On the other hand, Roy Hughes, the town's MP, was. He
indicated his support for a reduction in the age of consent to
eighteen but stopped at full equality at sixteen – indeed, in
1994, when Parliament debated reducing the age of consent, he
refused to support Edwina Currie's amendment to this effect.
Hughes was similarly supportive of the extension of gay rights
to Northern Ireland, Scotland, and military personnel, but, the
branch recorded in their newsletter *Rico-CHE*, he was 'obviously
terrified of being publicly associated with us'. Jeffrey Thomas,
MP for Abertillery, who defected to the Social Democratic Party
in 1981, was regarded by the branch as supportive of extended
gay rights. A similar position was taken by Neil Kinnock, MP
for Bedwellty, who 'sent the most favourable reply supporting
additional rights', although, similarly to Hughes, was concerned
that taking an open stance on gay rights in the Valleys might
be damaging electorally and so preferred 'such legislation to be
initiated by someone else'. That someone else was undoubtedly
Paul Flynn, who would be elected to Parliament in 1987. CHE
Newport regarded him as a hero, 'a man of courage and much
in sympathy with our cause. If all public figures were like him
the world would be a better place.'

Attitudes in the north of Wales were, at times, strikingly
different from those in Glamorgan and Monmouthshire. In the
summer of 1977, CHE Gwynedd met with North Wales Police
and the local probation service to discuss how the organisations

might work together. The probation service were understanding and recognised the need to co-operate, whereas the police
questioned the need to do so 'homosexuality being, they said, a
specifically English problem'.[59] Three years later, in 1980, Clwyd
County Council caused controversy when it implemented a total
ban on gay men and women working in any job where children
were involved – notably teaching and social services. When a
gay social worker was removed from his post by the council in
the spring of 1981, the local government trade union NALGO
sought legal advice as to whether they could challenge the ruling, but in the absence of anti-discrimination legislation were
told that the council had not acted improperly.[60] But in neighbouring Gwynedd, education officials explained to the National
Council for Civil Liberties that they 'would be prepared to employ
a teacher whom they knew to be homosexual and would not dis-
miss a teacher whom they discovered to be homosexual'.[61] The
council's director of social services had similarly given assurances
that gay men and women working in his department would not
face discrimination on the basis of sexual orientation.[62]

By the mid-1980s, the Sexual Offences Act was almost twenty
years old and its provisions together with unequal age of consent were the focus of an ongoing civil rights campaign. But in
comparison to London and other major cities in England and
Scotland, the Welsh contribution to that campaign now appeared
muted and largely depoliticised – there had been no pride march
and there was little indication that, the student movement aside,
any all-Wales campaigns were going to be established. The first
gay pride march held in Britain took place in London on 1 July
1972, around five years after the 1967 reform and three years
after the Stonewall riots in New York City. Bristol followed in
1977. It was not until 1985 that Wales had its first pride march,

although there had been isolated demonstrations before then such as at Mold in 1980 or the GLF march against unemployment in Cardiff in 1971.[63] Organised by students from UCC, the march took place on the afternoon of 20 June 1985 and passed by with relatively little comment and with almost no controversy in pages of the press.[64] One correspondent of the *South Wales Echo* wrote to the letters page quoting the infamous passages of Leviticus, but earned himself the mocking headline 'March of the Sinful Gays' and stern rebuttals from others who wrote stating that 'it is better to show love and compassion towards your fellow man than hate'.[65]

For Tim Foskett, one of the principal organisers, it was 'the right thing to do' at the right time. He drew on his childhood experiences of CND marches, which he attended with his mother, as well as his own experience of London Pride in 1984. The first two marches, in 1985 and 1986, started on Queen Street and ended up at the King's Cross, and were met with laughter and good will albeit that 'it felt like people were laughing at us', Foskett recalled. They found it 'humorous that we were walking down Queen Street'. For some of those marching there was undoubted nervousness at being completely visible. There were little bits of antagonism from onlookers, mostly confined to swearing, but no sign of more violent aggression – the most common reaction seems to have been a brief stare. Surviving footage showed the 1985 march led by the Cardiff GaySoc banner together with those from organisations such as Swansea Women's Centre, with participants handing out flyers and chanting 'We are everywhere.' The number of those marching increased steadily and by 1987 there were 'loads of us'. Cardiff's lesbians and gays were visible in a way that they had not been before: FRIEND was now regularly advertised in the *South Wales*

Echo and in the autumn of 1985 the *Echo* published its sympathetic exposé of the city's gay scene declaring Cardiff 'a place where you can be glad to be gay'.[66] Through their grit and determination a generation of activists had made it so.

Notes

1. *WM*, 5 September 1957.
2. *SWE*, 28 September 1966.
3. *SWE*, 30 October 1967.
4. Frank Mort, *Capital Affairs: London and the Making of the Permissive Society* (New Haven, 2010), p. 152.
5. Brian Lewis, *Wolfenden's Witnesses: Homosexuality in Postwar Britain* (London, 2016), p. 280, n. 2. TNA, HO 345/13, 31 March 1955, QQ1405-551. Watkins was similarly of the view that violence on television had made it 'a normal part of life'. *Sunday Times*, 29 January 1961. Higgins, *Heterosexual Dictatorship*, p. 122; Antony Grey, *Speaking Out: Writings on Sex, Law, Politics and Society, 1954–95* (London, 1997), p. 35
6. See TNA, HO 291/125: 'Homosexual offences known to the police in England and Wales, 1950–1961' and 'Persons against whom proceedings were taken in England and Wales in respect of homosexual offences, 1950–1961'.
7. *Western Mail*, 2 October 1957. See the similar comments made by the Revd Maldwyn Edwards in the *Western Mail* letters page, 9 September 1957.
8. *Western Mail*, 3 December 1957.
9. *Daily Mirror*, 11 September, 12 September 1957.
10. *The Manchester Guardian*, 11 September 1957.
11. *Western Mail*, 28 June 1958.
12. *Western Mail*, 20 August 1956.
13. As noted by Norena Shopland, *Forbidden Lives: LGBT Stories from Wales* (Bridgend, 2017).
14. E.g. *Daily Herald*, 30 June 1958; Higgins, *Heterosexual Dictatorship*, p. 126; Similar observations are made by Roger Davidson and Gayle Davis in their study of Scottish reactions to the Wolfenden Report. '"A Field for Private Members": The Wolfenden Committee and Scottish Homosexual Law Reform, 1950–1967', *Twentieth Century British History*, 15/2 (2004), 194.

15. *Daily Herald*, 29 April 1954.

16. See Donnelly's article, 'Blackmailer's Charter', *The Spectator*, 23 February 1962.

17. Sam Blaxland, 'Denbigh Constituency's First and Final Conservative MP: A Study of Geraint Morgan', *Transactions of the Denbighshire Historical Society*, 65 (2017), 87–100. Morgan viewed homosexual offences as a 'disagreeable subject'. *Liverpool Daily Post*, 23 December 1966. See also his column on 7 July 1967.

18. Marquand had been the MP for Cardiff East between 1945 and 1950.

19. Llywelyn Williams co-sponsored Abse's 1962 Sexual Offences Bill, for instance. Parliamentary Archives, HL/PO/PU/2/143. Sexual Offences Bill, 1962.

20. Leo Abse, 'Tidying Up the Law', *The Observer*, 4 March 1962.

21. HC Deb, 26 November 1958, vol. 596, cc. 486–9.

22. BBC Home Service, *What's the Idea?* (Broadcast: 17 August 1962). Transcript in TNA, HO 291/125.

23. W. Powell Phillips, *City and Port of Cardiff: Public Health Department, Annual Report for* 1969 (Cardiff, 1969), p. 93.

24. D. J. Anderson, *City and Port of Cardiff: Public Health Department, Annual Report for* 1972 (Cardiff, 1972), p. 100.

25. Lucy Robinson, *Gay Men and the Left in Post-war Britain: How the Personal Got Political* (Manchester, 2007).

26. *The Times*, 28 August 1971.

27. Robinson, *Gay Men*, 40.

28. See also Ray Davies's autobiography, *A Miner's Life* (Caerphilly, 2013).

29. Ray Davies, 'Pride: introductory speech given at the University of Glamorgan, Treforest, March 2015'. Available online: *https://www.youtube.com/watch?v=KkpOnX6DIKw* (accessed 25 May 2018); Ray Davies, *A Miner's Life* (Caerphilly, 2013).

30. This paragraph draws on Stephen Brooke's characterisation of the gay rights campaign within Labour in his *Sexual Politics: Sexuality, Family Planning and the British Left from the 1880s to the Present Day* (Oxford, 2011), p. 235.

31. *Lesbian and Gay Socialist* (Autumn, 1985), 13.

32. Evan Smith and Daryl Leeworthy, 'Before *Pride*: The Struggle for the Recognition of Gay Rights in the British Communist Movement, 1973–85', *Twentieth Century British History*, 27/4 (2016), 621–2.

33. Plaid Cymru, *Aims* (Cardiff, 1983), 10.

34. Plaid Cymru, *Youth Movement Handbook* (Cardiff, 1984), 6.

35. Mike Parker, 'Polls Apart', in John Osmond and Peter Finch (eds), *25/25 Vision: Welsh Horizons Across 50 Years* (Cardiff, 2012), 105.

36. S. A. Van Morgan, 'Plaid Cymru – The party of Wales: The new politics of Welsh Nationalism in the dawn of the 21st Century', in L. De Winter, M. Gómez-Reino, and P. Lynch (eds), *Autonomist Parties in Europe: Identity Politics and the Revival of the Territorial Cleavage* (Barcelona, 2006), 272.

37. Letter from Paul Templeton, CHE General Secretary, 9 February 1972 which gives details of the founding members of the branch.

38. *GR*, 9 November 1972.

39. Porter and Weeks, *Between The Acts*, p. 19. Fred's wider story is discussed in chapter two.

40. See, for instance, Sue Bruley's letter in *Gay Left* 3 (1976).

41. *GN* 11 (14 November 1972).

42. *GN* 16 (7 February 1973).

43. Letter, 11 October 1972; Tim Foskett observed that the university's GaySoc was still absent lesbians when he started attending in 1984. *GR*, 24 October 1984.

44. CHE Gwynedd Newssheet, 19 (October 1977).

45. Deirdre Beddoe, *Out of the Shadows: A History of Women in Twentieth Century Wales* (Cardiff, 2000), p. 163.

46. GA, DWAW/6/1: Cardiff Women's Newsletter, July 1981; September/October 1981.

47. Leeds Gay Liberation Society, *Broadsheet* 4 (February 1972), 3.

48. *Broadsheet* (Cardiff), 21 October 1971.

49. Leeds Gay Liberation Society, *Broadsheet* 3 (December 1971); 4 (February 1972).

50. Interview with Antoinette Lorraine, 7 December 2016. Available online: *https://www.youtube.com/watch?v=JLsiv7vB8m8* (Accessed 25 May 2018). The interview was produced for the VCS Chronicle project.

51. Email correspondence to the author from Joanie Slatoff, 19 January 2017.

52. *Broadsheet* 12 (December 1972). Activity did not improve until early 1974. See *Broadsheet* 23 (February–March 1974).

53. *GN* 1 (1 May 1972); *Broadsheet* 17 (June 1973); Polly Blue, 'A time to refrain from embracing' in Linda Hurcombe (ed.), *Sex and God* (London, 1987), 69.

54. *Broadsheet* 18 (August 1973).

55. *Broadsheet* 17 (June 1973); 19 (October 1973); 23 (February–March 1974).

56. LSE Archives, Programme for the 1st Wales Gay Rights Conference, University College of North Wales, Bangor, 23–24 November 1974; Tim Foskett, 'Interview Notes'.

57. The organisation had previously been known as the LGB Forum Cymru, which was established by the Welsh Assembly in August 2001.

58. *GN* 61 (1974), 23; CHE, *Bulletin* (1974).

59. CHE Gwynedd Newssheet 17 (August 1977).

60. *Evening Leader* (Wrexham), 22 July, 23 July, 20 October 1980; *Liverpool Post*, 12 August 1980, 9 May 1981.

61. CHE Gwynedd Newssheet 19 (October 1977).

62. CHE Gwynedd Newssheet 8 (November 1976).

63. *Evening Leader*, 15 December 1980.

64. *GR*, 12 June 1985.

65. *SWE*, 20 May, 28 May 1985.

66. *SWE*, 20 November 1985.

CHAPTER SIX

A Lost World?

In April 1985, more than 12,000 health workers in South Glamorgan received a letter alongside their monthly pay packet offering advice and reassurance about HIV/AIDS. The letter came amidst growing anxiety about the illness and the perceived threat to staff working at clinics in the county and particularly at the University Hospital of Wales. 'There has been concern and alarm in the population and among health staff', observed a spokesperson, 'and we felt it essential that everyone working for the health authority be reassured'.[1] Two years earlier in January 1983, a young man aged just twenty, who was other-wise being treated for haemophilia, presented with symptoms that were eventually diagnosed as AIDS related. During clinical investigations, it became apparent that the blood used to treat his haemophilia, imported from the United States to mitigate low blood stocks in the UK, had been infected. When the *Mail on Sunday* broke the news in May 1983, Cardiff became the focus of intense media scrutiny.[2] The headlines were alarmist. AIDS was designated 'the Gay Plague', a label already applied in the United States, and the question of 'tainted blood' became a national scandal. Senior officials rushed to deny the plausibility of patients becoming infected through blood transfusions.[3] In reality, the earliest AIDS-related deaths in the city were the result of precisely that: transfusions of infected blood.[4]

The 1980s and 1990s were undoubtedly a difficult period, with the advent of the HIV/AIDS epidemic, the introduction of Section 28, and the failure to bring about equalisation of the age of consent in 1994. The decline of the political activism of the 1970s and increasing commercialisation of gay culture as society became more tolerant also encouraged a sense of nostalgia for the more 'authentic' ways of living of the 1970s. But how much of a change was registered in Wales during this period? There were outbursts of anxiety about HIV/AIDS, but with relatively few cases of infection, such incidents can easily imply a much stronger sense of public hysteria than was the case. Likewise, the high-profile campaign against Clause 28 in the first half of 1988 needs to be set against both its implementation (or otherwise) by local councils and the longer-term absence of effective information about LGBT matters in schools across Wales. And what of homophobia more generally? These themes provide the contours of this chapter, which seeks a nuanced understanding of the gay and lesbian experience in Thatcher's Wales.

Early in 1985, a cleaners' strike at the Taliesin Theatre at University College Swansea symbolised public confusion about HIV/AIDS. After a five-year absence from Wales, the theatre group Gay Sweatshop were due to perform their play *Poppies*.[5] Behind the scenes, the theatre's cleaning staff had raised concerns about the risk of catching HIV/AIDS and asked for additional protective clothing, rubber gloves, disinfectant and other materials they regarded as essential for their safety at work.[6] When the request was refused by the Taliesin's director, the cleaners went on strike. Articles in the tabloid press offered support to the cleaners, although as one member of Gay Sweatshop pointed out 'the chances of sex between the women and the actors is remote, to say the least'.[7] It turned out that the cleaners had been manipulated for the sake of publicity and in the weeks afterwards the student union at Swansea debated a motion of censure in the theatre's director.[8] He denied the claim, but the censure was passed regardless.[9]

A few months later, UCS was again the focus of a discrimination dispute when a first-year physics student was asked to delay his matriculation because he was a haemophiliac and the university were concerned about how they could support him. Although the university and the physics department denied they were making direct links between haemophilia and AIDS, this was exactly how the student and the student union read the situation. Defending the official stance, the college's assistant registrar explained that if the illness 'came out into the open' it could create 'a scare' and the delay in registration would therefore provide the authorities with enough time to come up with appropriate support.[10] The debacle prompted the student union to adopt a formal AIDS policy in January 1986 noting that 'the lack of policy may severely impair our ability to respond and advise in the event of one of our members contracting AIDS'.

With their new policy in place, the student union organised the first AIDS awareness week at Swansea, became more resolute in their LGBT activism and more determined in their campaigns against homophobia, sexism and racism on campus. Homophobic material was banned from the student union and *Gay Times* was stocked in the student union shop, although not without difficulties. Staff members occasionally expressed outrage at the contents and the covers and refused to sell it to students.[11]

What happened within Swansea in 1985–86 was indicative of the missteps taken by public bodies in response to HIV/AIDS, often because of extreme caution rather than any overt homophobic hysteria. In the autumn of 1986, the Welsh Rugby Union ordered all adult players to be screened for HIV/AIDS because the scrum was believed to be an obvious point of infection.[12] Similar anxiety led to the issue of notices at leisure centres and swimming pools declaring that HIV/AIDS sufferers were banned from facilities run by the Sports Council for Wales, most notably the National Sports Centre in Sophia Gardens, Cardiff.[13] In the north, Arfon Borough Council adopted a similar stance by banning anyone with HIV/AIDS from using its swimming pools, although as one councillor noted 'we are the only council in the whole of Wales imposing this restriction'.[14] Had there been a more widespread panic, bans on the use of leisure facilities would have been imposed by all local authorities, but this was not the case. Instead, there was an emphasis on public health and education. Awareness weeks were organised at universities, part of a national campaign organised by the NUS to break down the popular association between HIV/AIDS and 'gay plague'. Education videos such as 'Let's See What Tomorrow Brings' were also created, and training was provided by public health experts to health workers, educators and those in social services.[15] As Colin Griffiths of West Glamorgan's Health Education Unit noted in 1986, 'we hope this direct approach will temper the anxiety about AIDS which is obviously present but, hopefully, will be shown not to be justified'.[16] Griffiths became a leading advocate of a public health response to the spread of HIV/AIDS and was appointed director of the Welsh AIDS Campaign on its foundation towards the end of 1986. He used his experience of information training in

West Glamorgan as the basis of Wales-wide initiatives.[17] These included the first AIDS information leaflet produced anywhere in Britain targeted at school children, which was published bilingually in 1987, and the high-profile *Survey on Knowledge of AIDS in Wales*.[18]

The survey showed that as many as a quarter of the Welsh population thought that kissing placed a person at high risk of infection and that nearly 60 per cent of Welsh men believed 'it was their own fault if homosexuals and drug addicts got AIDS and did not feel sorry for them'. Nearly 50 per cent of women held the same view. Fatalistically, one in three people in Wales thought nothing could be done to prevent infection.[19] In Griffiths's view, the government-funded national information campaign, including the infamous tombstone advert 'don't die of ignorance' had succeeded only 'in panicking those who are not at risk and switching off those who are'. Confusion reigned. As Griffiths explained,

> One caller to the Welsh Helpline had asked if AIDS could be contracted through eating raw black pudding ... This may appear amusing, but it illustrates the point that people draw their own conclusions when presented with information. AIDS is transmitted in blood; black pudding is made from dried blood. Asking if he could catch AIDS seemed a logical question.[20]

With this in mind, there is little wonder that the Taliesin cleaners had asked for extra gloves and cleaning fluids.

In 1987, the Welsh Office merged the Welsh AIDS Campaign into the Health Advisory Committee for Wales (later the Health Promotion Authority for Wales) sacrificing the targeted efficacy of the campaign for 'coherence' and budgetary efficiency. As Victoria Berridge noted in the 1990s, the Welsh AIDS Campaign 'sank without trace'.[21] In retrospect, this decision should be one of regret. The replacement *Healthy Sexuality* programme focused less on dissemination of knowledge to targeted groups and more on raising public awareness of sexually transmitted infections generally, as well as sex education and safe sex promotion amongst young people, drug users and prostitutes.[22] Unsurprisingly, *Healthy Sexuality* had little meaningful impact on public attitudes towards HIV/AIDS. Even into the early 1990s, over half of men and women in Wales agreed with the statement 'I don't feel sorry for homosexuals infected with HIV because it is their own fault'.[23] In such an environment, some car drivers willingly displayed stickers declaring 'Stop AIDS: Run Over A Queer'.[24] During UCC's AIDS awareness week in February 1988, Tim Foskett discussed his own experiences:

> Nearly three years ago, in the middle of June 1985, lesbians and gay men in Wales walked down the streets of Cardiff in the first Welsh Lesbian and Gay Pride March. Many of us gave out leaflets, explaining the point of the march to the onlookers. Most of them seemed a bit shocked at first, but countered their ignorance with a smile or even a laugh. The vast majority took a leaflet.
>
> Two years later, June 1987 saw the third Welsh Lesbian and Gay Pride March. Things had definitely changed. There was fear in the faces of the onlookers. This time very few laughed and many moved away as we approached them with a leaflet. About 40 people told us that we should be sent to the gas ovens.[25]

But how widespread was HIV/AIDS in Wales in the 1980s? Epidemiological figures are difficult to use, and contemporary estimates often came with several caveats attached as to their accuracy.[26] In South Glamorgan, the county with the highest rates of HIV/AIDS infection in Wales, just 4 cases had been identified by the summer of 1986 (3 of whom had died) – a very small proportion of the 350 cases nationwide at the time. Just 14 cases had been identified by the end of 1989.[27] As late as 1997, Iechyd Morgannwg, then the health board for Swansea, Neath and Port Talbot, noted that just 40 people had been diagnosed with HIV/AIDS in West Glamorgan, of whom 26 had died. By that time more than 9,000 out of the more than 13,000 reported cases across Britain had died in the 16 years since the first infection was recorded in December 1981.[28] 'Wales in general, and perhaps South Glamorgan in particular has been spared, somewhat strangely', reflected one doctor in 1987. He continued:

> the rapid advance of AIDS as witnessed in other parts of the United Kingdom ... The position is reminiscent of the 'phoney war' during the last months of 1939 and advantage is being taken ... to prepare the Authority's counselling and health promotion services for the heavy tasks which lie ahead.[29]

Such low levels of infection had important effects on public organisation. Student groups and some gay bars worked to provide condoms through the installation of machines or through free distribution.[30] But local authorities and health authorities, except for South and West Glamorgan and Gwent, were slow in establishing hospice care, helplines and dedicated counselling teams.[31] In Cardiff, where the service was relatively comprehensive, these eventually came under the umbrella of SGAN – the South Glamorgan AIDS Network.[32] The first of Wales's official helplines, Cardiff AIDS Helpline, launched in July 1986 with funding from South Glamorgan Health Authority, although it built on an earlier initiative run by community volunteers from Cardiff FRIEND.[33] A counselling service followed in 1987.[34] Gwent AIDS Helpline came into existence in 1987 through the auspices of the Gwent Centre for Health Promotion.[35] The Mid Glamorgan AIDS Helpline was not set up until the 1990s. Until then those with HIV/AIDS in much of the Valleys were directed to services intended either for drug users, or to social services.[36]

Health education undoubtedly provided for a more nuanced understanding of HIV/AIDS, despite the paucity of facilities in large parts of Wales. By 1989, doctors in Cardiff expressed the hope that 'society is now learning to live sensibly with AIDS in our midst' and that the public had moved from 'reactive' to 'proactive' ways of dealing with the crisis. 'This means', argued Donald Anderson, the city's consultant of public health medicine, 'developing responsible attitudes, adopting protective lifestyles, and remaining very much alive to the potential hazards ahead ... It does not mean complacency'.[37] Perhaps ironically, given popular perceptions of danger and historical association, the rates of infection in the 2000s and 2010s were far higher than in the 1980s and early 1990s. Whereas the number of new AIDS cases has declined and remained low, HIV infections have increased particularly because of transmission between men and women.[38] Most of the facilities and advice lines established to provide support in the 1980s and 1990s have also closed down.

The emergence of HIV/AIDS provided an excuse for social conservatives to try to reverse the development of a public gay culture in the 1970s and early 1980s. During the 1987 general election, several Conservative Party candidates in Wales expressed overtly homophobic opinions to benefit from a perceived public appetite for more stringent restrictions on homosexual activity. The declarations were stark and vicious, ramped up for effect. In Pontypridd, Desmond Swayne complained that the government had not done enough to protect the wider public against the spread of HIV/AIDS and as a precautionary measure should imprison all gays and lesbians. His Labour counterpart Brynmor John dismissed the idea as ridiculous fantasy.[39] In Newport East, Graham Webster-Gardiner declared the AIDS information campaign a 'waste of money'.[40] Webster-Gardiner had already made something of a name for himself as the chair of the Conservative Family Campaign, a pressure group committed to the recriminalisation of homosexuality, internment of AIDS patients, and removal of public funding for organisations such as the Terrence Higgins Trust and the Family Planning Association.

In Swansea East, Richard Lewis used his election campaign to amplify what was already a deeply hostile stance. The *Uplands Newsletter*, which was linked to his campaign and had already contained articles declaring that readers should not eat food cooked by homosexuals, now branded gay students at UCS as perverts and blamed them for helping to spread HIV/AIDS in the city through sexual promiscuity.[41] None of these men could defeat their Labour opponents and in each constituency the Conservatives showed a slight decrease in the share of the vote compared with the 1983 general election, but the Thatcher government returned to office. Victory enabled further remodelling of Britain's public services, implementation of a vigorous programme of privatisation ranging from the sale of British Airways to public utilities, and the introduction of the 'internal market' into the National Health Service. The general election also marked a clear socially conservative turn, despite its rejection at the ballot box in many parts of Wales. It was signalled by the now infamous speech given by Margaret Thatcher to the Conservative Party Conference in October 1987 in which she derided the idea that children were being taught that they 'have an inalienable right to be gay'.

Taking their cue, two backbench MPs David Wilshire and Jill Knight, proposed a new clause for the Local Government Bill in early December. Its aim was to outlaw the 'promotion of homosexuality'. Enthusiastically adopted by the government, the clause prompted a fierce public campaign led by the quickly established Organisation for Lesbian and Gay Action (OLGA) to prevent its implementation. The local campaign, Wales Against Clause 28, was co-ordinated by Tim Foskett, who was by then general secretary of UCC Student Union and the most prominent gay student activist in Wales. He ran the campaign from his office in Cathays Park. The first march and rally organised by Wales Against Clause 28 was held in Cardiff on 30 January 1988. More than 500 people gathered in Cathays Park despite threats of violence and intimidation from the National Front – who had leafleted parts of the city such as Roath and Cathays with material declaring 'smash gay demo' and 'do you hate queers?' – to listen to speeches from Peter Tatchell, Alun Davies (then president of NUS Wales), and student union sabbatical officers from Cardiff and Bangor. Letters of support were read aloud from David Steel, then leader of the Liberal Party; Chris Smith, Britain's first openly gay MP; the Wales TUC, and the EastEnders actor Michael Cashman.[42]

Amongst the many placards carried on the march through the city centre – from outside the law courts through

Queen Street and onwards to the Hayes – were signs identifying the places the mainly lesbian and gay marchers had lived and where they were from to disprove the popular notion that 'there were no gays in Wales'. Despite the hostility evident at the gay pride march six months earlier, this march took place on a busy Saturday afternoon with shoppers looking on. There was support from Cardiff Trades Council and several political parties. The National Front, who turned up in small numbers to harass the march, were easily contained by the police. A further rally held in Bangor on 23 February coincided with the campus Lesbian and Gay Awareness Day, and was attended by nearly 200 protestors. Speeches were given by students, members of the local theatre and arts scene and representatives of the Church in Wales. At the end, several hundred pink balloons were released 'as a sign of our outrage at this sort of legislation which is written in the language of bar room bigotry not the language of the law'.[43]

Further action took place in early April as part of the 'national days of local action'. These included picketing of the South Glamorgan County Council offices and a further march through the streets of Cardiff. In an interview with *Gair Rhydd*, Tim Foskett declared that 'we demand equality before the law and within the workplace; we demand that local authorities are receptive to the needs of lesbian and gay constituents'.[44] But the campaign found it difficult to engage directly with councillors, and activists were denied access to county hall. Attention steadily turned to the national rally in London scheduled for 30 April. In advance, Hywel Francis wrote to Mike Jackson of LGSM to record 'the wholehearted support of the Neath, Dulais and Swansea Valley Miners' Support Group in your and our present struggle against the anti-gay legislation. As you told us in the miners' strike – "your struggle is our struggle"'. More than 30,000 people attended the London rally, although at the time estimates were even as high as 50,000. Together with the 20,000 strong demonstration in Manchester on 20 February, these were the largest gay protests in British history – but they failed to stop the clause.

Or did they? To what extent was Section 28 actively implemented by local government? Anecdotally, Section 28 had a stark effect. Writing in *Union Eyes*, the newsletter of Cardiff Trades Council, Tim Foskett observed its rapid implementation across Britain: 'Reports of physical attacks have increased four-fold in the last two years', he noted, and 'overt prejudice towards lesbians and gay men has now received a new credibility because of Clause 28'. He continued:

> Already libraries are removing books by lesbian and gay authors, theatres are hesitant about which productions they will take, councils have stopped work intended to investigate the needs of this section of the population, and teachers have been threatened with dismissal if they admit that they are gay.[45]

There were occasional scuffles in Wales following the law's introduction: in Aberystwyth, part of an exhibition was removed from the town's library on the basis that it contravened the local government act. The items removed included an advert for local gay discos and an advert for a gay Asian befriending service. In protest, three activists stormed the town library, two of whom chained themselves to a radiator. Council officials insisted that 'it was illegal for local government to knowingly promote lesbianism or homosexuality' and had no choice to act as they did.[46] Councillors themselves seem to have paid little direct attention to the implications of the legislation.[47] But such incidents were isolated. In West Glamorgan, Conservative members of the council pressed the ruling Labour group to declare that homosexual acts were 'self-evidently unnatural' and to remove any support for gay initiatives. They refused, amidst cries Labour were 'pampering to the poofs'.[48]

The introduction of the 1993 Education Act had some mitigating effects on the way Section 28 operated since it placed into the sex education curriculum the need to teach about HIV/AIDS and placed responsibility for developing sex education policy into the hands of a school's governing body. Amongst some LEAs, that meant writing sex education policies consistent with the 'non-promotion' stipulated in Section 28, whereas others provided more freedom. In Mid Glamorgan, indicatively, guidelines introduced into schools in the mid-1990s suggested that 'schools should not ... present homosexuality as the norm, advocate homosexuality or encourage sexual experimentation by pupils'.[49] In 2000, the *Western Mail* surveyed all education authorities in Wales about their implementation of Section 28 and received a range of replies pointing to the divergence of opinion across the country. There was a stark response from directors of education in Powys and Monmouthshire who stated that their authorities expected 'all schools to follow Section 28 of the Local Government Act'. Whereas in Blaenau Gwent, the director of education pointed out that 'of course homosexuality is going to be discussed; children have inquisitive minds'. Similar comments were made by directors of education from Bridgend, Neath Port Talbot, Rhondda Cynon Taf, and Swansea.[50]

The deliberate homophobia of Section 28 provided for a renewal of the civil rights campaign, which had waned since the heyday of the GLF and CHE in the early 1970s and led to the launch of Stonewall in London in 1989. There was fresh debate about equality and civil liberties, about equalisation of consent and education, and a sense that society should act to prevent the ongoing violence and harassment that many LGBT people faced. Although homophobic attacks had somewhat abated since the 1960s, they had not disappeared (and still have not). In 1995, Stonewall published a report on homophobia in Britain, which noted that as many as one in three gay people living in Wales had suffered from violence and harassment. The recorded figure for young people under eighteen was more than 50 per cent.[51] These figures have remained stubbornly fixed. Over half of young people, according to Stonewall Cymru's 2003 report, recorded being bullied or physically intimidated. In 2007, a fifth of respondents explained that they had experienced some form of homophobic incident in the past twelve months, mostly of a casual nature. The 2017 report, despite considerable advances in civil rights legislation, not least civil partnerships and gay marriage, recorded similar figures.

The obvious question to ask is why? Why in the face of significant enhancements in civil liberties has homophobia remained stubbornly present in Welsh society? In part, the answer lies in the historical weakness of the gay rights movement in most of Wales. Welsh members of Parliament (almost entirely from the Labour benches) were at the forefront of political change in the second half of the twentieth century: from Desmond Donnelly's call for a royal commission in 1954 to Neil Kinnock's impassioned plea for equalisation of the age of consent forty years later. But this was not always mirrored at the local level and in many respects the growth of CHE and GLF in the 1970s was unusual. There are also difficult questions to answer about the relationship between queer identities and national identities – hardly a dilemma unique to Wales. Absence of a visible culture connected in some way to local circumstances has, nevertheless, made that relationship more difficult even as national symbols – the dragon, in particular – have been co-opted as symbols of Pride.

This co-option is novel, for historically there has been a sense that homosexuality and Welshness (in all its forms) were at odds with each other. The telephone logs of Cardiff FRIEND carried indicative notes of several conversations from gay people in the 1970s and 1980s who struggled to reconcile being Welsh and gay. Some regarded it as part of the 'Anglicisation process' and the steady loss of their Welshness as they came out. As the logs recorded of one discussion, 'being gay to him was no problem in England but in Wales he had to live two separate lives'. The volunteer noted 'I have come across this before'. Likewise, during the debate on Section 28 in 1988, one group of students at Bangor complained in the campus newspaper that

> The use of the Welsh dragon [on anti-Clause campaign literature] caused extensive offence and anger amongst Welsh students who feel that its association with homosexuality is a slur on their nationality and who believe that their symbol of national pride should be left out of such contentious and personal campaigns.[52]

Such distinctions make for difficult reading, but queer identity and national identity have historically been uncomfortably juxtaposed in most western contexts. Wales is hardly unique.

It is, in retrospect, easy to feel a sense of nostalgia for earlier periods of activity, but there is also a need to be cautious. The absence of activity and organisation in the twenty-first century is not necessarily the result of decline but the persistence of nothing. Thus, at the Polytechnic of Wales in Pontypridd, now the University of South Wales, there was almost no organisation of lesbian and gay students in the 1970s and 1980s, although there was a strong anti-sexism group which led on women's rights.[53] At the start of the 1980s, the student union stated in its handbook that 'subject to demand it is hoped a GaySoc will be established to facilitate some provision for gay students, which has been sadly lacking in the past'. No mention was made of its existence until 1989.[54] Similarly, at University College Swansea the student union tried for several years – through the 1980s and into the 1990s – to secure direct lesbian and gay representation on their executive. However, the attempts were consistently opposed by the university's governing body and the principal.[55]

In fact, in December 1991 the student union noted a steady increase of overt and subtle homophobia on campus not least intimidation, verbal and physical harassment, the tearing down of lesbian and gay-related posters, the theft of a rainbow flag marking Lesbian, Gay and Bisexual Awareness Week, and the deliberate vandalism of the LGB noticeboard 'every week so far this term'. The absence of college support for lesbian, gay and bisexual initiatives was regarded as tantamount to official encouragement of homophobia and low-level violence. For all that the student union sought to inculcate an inclusive environment on campus, together with liberally-minded lecturers in the arts and humanities and social sciences, their efforts were frustrated by a conservative administration. Nor was this solely the view of the students. When a civil engineering lecturer complained in the UCS newsletter in 1987 that the 'college has been distinctly associated with pro-gay activities and activists' and that the time had come to 'disassociate' from such 'biologically abnormal' practices, it sparked nearly six months of furious debate across campus.[56] Lecturers from across the university denounced not only the correspondent but also the principal whose stance on free speech earned plaudits from the Conservative Party but the scorn of many of his colleagues.[57]

In a stark letter, several lecturers at UCS, including M. Wynn Thomas and the future vice chancellor of Cardiff University, Colin Riordan, who was then a lecturer in the modern languages faculty, warned that

> It seems to us that the principal's defence of the right to free speech should be accompanied by public dissociation of our university from such provocatively illiberal views. For we do not teach, or wish to teach, in such an illiberal university, nor live, or wish to live, in such an illiberal society as seem to be aimed at by the councillor in question.[58]

The councillor in question was Richard Lewis, a maverick conservative who had declared his regret that the 1967 Sexual Offences Act had been passed. It was, he said, the 'biggest mistake this country ever made'.[59] Lewis had also taken advantage of an invitation by the UCS Conservative Association to speak on campus to demand that homosexual teachers and lecturers be sacked.[60] When the principal defended Lewis's right to free speech and threatened protesting students with expulsion and a drama lecturer with the sack, the student union condemned 'the Principal, Professor Clarkson for his complicity' in what it regarded as a homophobic campaign and organised a protest of its own. At least a hundred students chanted 'Clarkson Out!'[61] He eventually retired in 1994. A quarter of a century later, Swansea University ranks amongst the best workplaces in Britain on Stonewall's equality index. The same index places

Cardiff University fourteenth and the National Assembly for Wales at the top.

The efforts by those such as Richard Lewis to reverse the expansion of civil rights for minorities have largely failed, then, with substantial legislative progress taking place over the past two decades. The age of consent was equalised at sixteen years of age in 2000. Section 28 was abolished in 2003. The following year, the Labour government introduced the Gender Recognition Act, enabling transgender men and women to assert their own gender identity, and the Civil Partnership Act mirroring similar legislation on the continent that enabled gay couples to have quasi-civil marriage. Equal marriage was introduced by the Coalition government in 2013. Alongside, and in common with pride events elsewhere in Britain, there has been tremendous growth in the number of people taking part in Pride Cymru. Launched as Cardiff Mardi Gras in 1999, with five thousand people taking part, the festival now has an annual audience of fifty thousand. Rainbow flags – and rainbow dragons – are far more visible than they have ever been.

*

But what of queer Wales? To what extent are historical experiences reflected in the apparent ease with which identities are expressed by contemporary society? And what does advancing our knowledge of Wales's queer history bring to our wider understanding of Wales and the Welsh, past and present? Circumstances in the twenty-first century undoubtedly provide very different experiences and expressions of sexuality from those of the medieval, early modern, Victorian, or twentieth century periods. In those earlier times, as this book has shown, lesbian, gay and queer sexualities were characterised by their absence from the spoken and written record, except by allusion or by the intermittent appearance of the unlucky in crime records. Men had sex with other men in dockland hostels, on mountainsides in the valleys, or on the secluded beaches of the west. They cruised and cottaged or sought the safety of a car or the back of a taxicab. They did not (apparently) discriminate based on race or age or language. None of this was peculiarly Welsh, of course, and in most respects the Welsh experience was akin to that of the north of England, where class and live and let live tolerances were strong.

Yet in the years since devolution and the establishment of national campaign groups such as Stonewall Cymru and Pride Cymru it has become more straightforward to write about queer Wales in the singular, rather than to reflect on regional variations and the interconnectivity of Welsh LGBT activism within a wider British (or more often English and Welsh) network. Pride Cymru, for instance, is more obviously Welsh than was Cardiff CHE. This suggests a change in recent years, as the juxtaposition between Welshness and sexual and gender diversity has lost its historical 'awkwardness', and the absence of activism has been replaced by public celebration and visible diversity. Perhaps, then, queer Wales lies ahead not behind, in the future and not the past.

Notes

1. *SWE*, 1 May 1985.

2. *Mail on Sunday*, 1 May 1983.

3. Although concern about infection from transfusion grew steadily, with two students from UCS banned for donating in 1986 because they were lesbians. *SWEP*, 14 November 1986. The National Blood Transfusion Service later apologised. Nor was it merely blood that was affected, for the spread of HIV/AIDS amongst women had a clear impact on provision of human milk in maternity wards. Cardiff Community Health Council, *Annual Report, 1987* (Cardiff, 1987).

4. J. F. Skone, *The Health Services in South Glamorgan during 1985* (Cardiff, 1986); J. F. Skone, *The Health Services in South Glamorgan during 1986* (Cardiff, 1987), 46.

5. *DT*, 11 February 1985.

6. *SWEP*, 8 February 1985; *The Stage*, 7 March 1985; NLW, HTV Wales Archive, 'Wales at Six: 19 February 1985'.

7. *The Sun*, 19 February 1985.

8. *DT*, 25 February 1985.

9. *DT*, 11 March 1985.

10. *DT*, 18 November 1985.

11. Richard Burton Archives, 2011/27/7, Swansea Student Union, General Policy File, 1984–1994: AIDS Campaign, 22 January 1986; Lesbian and Gay Rights, 19 February 1986. 2011/27/4, General Council Minutes, 1987–1988: 10 November 1987.

12. *GR*, 10 December 1986.

13. *SWDP*, 13 December 1986. Nor were they alone in this kind of reaction. In December 1986 the *Gay Times* reported that a producer for BBC Wales had been reprimanded for broadcasting a programme on AIDS that contained 'coarse' and 'earthy' language. *Gay Times*, December 1986, 7. Cited in David Trevor Evans, *Sexual Citizenship: The Material Construction of Sexualities* (London, 1993), 285, n. 26.

14. *Seren*, 25 May 1987.

15. J. F. Skone, *The Health Services in South Glamorgan during 1987* (Cardiff, 1988), 177–8; *DT*, 10 March 1986; *Seren*, 27 January 1986

16. Colin Griffiths, Elizabeth Cruse, Joan Harries, Toni Williams, and B.N.C. Littlepage, 'AIDS – A Health Education Approach in West Glamorgan', *Health Education Journal*, 44/4 (1985), 172–3.

17. Third International Conference on Acquired Immunodeficiency Syndrome (AIDS), Abstracts Book, June 1987, 38. The broadest study of the Welsh AIDS Campaign can be found in V. Blakey, R. Parish and D. Reid, 'Health Promotion Responses to AIDS in Wales: The Welsh AIDS Campaign', in Maryan Pye, Mukesh Kapila, Graham Buckley and Deirdre Cunningham (eds), *Responding to the AIDS Challenge: A Comparative Study of Local AIDS Programmes in the United Kingdom* (London, 1989).

18. *Union Eyes* 5 (October 1987), 6; *The Observer*, 1 February 1987. Welsh AIDS Campaign, *AIDS: What It Means For Young People* (Cardiff, 1987). A copy of the survey is held at the Glamorgan Archives, where it was consulted. GA, Mid Glamorgan County Council Records, MD/C/X/6.

19. Don Nutbeam, John C. Catford, Simon A. Smail and Colin Griffiths, 'Public Knowledge and Attitudes to AIDS', *Public Health* 103 (1989), 205–211.

20. *Chemist & Druggist*, 17 October 1987.

21. Virginia Berridge, *AIDS in the UK: The Making of a Policy, 1981–1994* (Oxford, 1996), 126.

22. Health Promotion Authority for Wales, *Strategic Directions for the Health Promotion Authority for Wales* (Cardiff, 1990).

23. C. Roberts, V. Blakey, and C. Smith 'Changes in Public Knowledge and Attitudes to HIV/AIDS in Wales, 1987 to 1992', *AIDS Care*, 6/4 (1994).

24. I am grateful to Matt Cook for this information which draws on his study of Mass Observation. See his 'AIDS, Mass Observation, and the Fate of the Permissive Turn', *Journal of the History of Sexuality*, 26/2 (2017), 239–272; and '"Archives of Feeling": The AIDS Crisis in Britain, 1987', *History Workshop Journal*, 83/1 (2017), 51–78.

25. *GR*, 10 February 1988.

26. West Glamorgan Health Authority, *Health in West Glamorgan, 1991* (Swansea, 1991), 10.

27. Skone, *Health Services 1985*, 183; South Glamorgan Health Authority, *The Health of South Glamorgan in 1990* (Cardiff, 1990), 24. Although as the report noted the figure did 'not reflect the true position in the County because of patient mobility into, and out of the area. This led to a heavier patient load than the figures suggest'.

28. Iechyd Morgannwg, *Report '97: Report of the Director of Public Health* (Swansea, 1997), 31–32. See also, Olwen E. Williams, 'HIV Ac AIDS: Y Sefyllfa yng Nghymru', *Cennad: Cylchgrawn y Gymdeithas Feddygol*, 14 (1995), 68–76.

29. Skone, *Health Services 1986*, 170. Indeed, a major study published in 1988 noted that just 4 per cent of gay men had been infected in Wales, whereas in London infection rates were as high as 14 per cent. *SWE*, 1 December 1988; *WM*, 1 December 1988; Peter M. Davies et al., *Sex, Gay Men and AIDS* (London, 1993), 99.

30. NLW, HTV Archive, 'News Material, 20 March 1987'.

31. Cardiff Community Health Council, *Annual Report, 1986* (Cardiff, 1986).

32. South Glamorgan Health Authority, *District HIV Co-ordinating Centre: Uniting Care and Prevention into the 90s* (Cardiff, n.d.); South Glamorgan Health Authority, *Positive Steps: A Guide to Care Services for People Affected by HIV/AIDS in South Glamorgan* (Cardiff, n.d.).

33. CLS, *AIDS Helpline, Annual Reports 1989, 1990, 1994–5*.

34. GA, DX881/15, *South Glamorgan AIDS Newsletter, 1988*. This became *South Glamorgan AIDS Review* in the 1990s. See CLS for issues 2 and 3 (1991, 1992) and Bro Taf HIV/AIDS Review for 1995–2001.

35. *Druglink* 2/3 (May–June 1987), 15.

36. Mid Glamorgan County Council, *Positive Steps for People Affected by HIV/ AIDS: A Guide to Services, Advice and Counselling in Mid Glamorgan* (Bridgend, 1990).

37. Donald Anderson, 'Learning to Live with AIDS', in J. F. Skone, *The Health Services in South Glamorgan during 1988* (Cardiff, 1989), 219-220.

38. Public Health Wales, *HIV and STI Trends in Wales: Surveillance Report, March 2011* (Cardiff: Public Health Wales, 2011).

39. *Pontypridd Observer*, 27 November, 4 December 1986.

40. *SWA*, 1 December 1986.

41. *WM*, 12 December 1986; *Bad Press*, 3 February 1987.

42. LSE Archives, HCA/EPHEMERA/370, 'Leaflet for a march organised in Cardiff'. The rally was attended by the campaigner Peter Tatchell. Extracts from his speech are held at the LSE. See HCA/TATCHELL/1992/5; *Spare Rib*, 190 (May 1988), 39. *GR*, 3 February 1988.

43. *Seren: The UCNW Student Magazine*, 27 February 1988.

44. *Spare Rib*, 190 (May 1988), 39; *GR*, 20 April 1988.

45. Tim Foskett, 'Clause 28: A Trade Union Issue', *Union Eyes*, 3/3 (Summer 1988), 1.

46. *Cambrian News*, 5 February, 26 August 1988, 2 June 1989; *WM*, 29 May 1989.

47. *Cambrian News*, 22 July 1988.

48. *WM*, 19 August 1988; *SWEP*, 20 August, 19 October 1988; *Gay Times* (February 1988).

49. *SWE*, 16 April 1993.

50. *WM*, 11 February 2000.

51. *WM*, 30 November 1995.

52. *Seren*, 7 March 1988.

53. Polytechnic of Wales, *Student Union Handbook, 1982–1983* (Pontypridd, 1982), p. 50.

54. Polytechnic of Wales, *Student Union Handbook, 1981–1982* (Pontypridd, 1981), p. 71; Polytechnic of Wales, *Student Union Handbook, 1989–1990* (Pontypridd, 1989). The group seems to have existed by 1987. See, GA, FRIEND South Wales, Telephone Logs, October 1987.

55. *BP*, 10 March 1987. The wider point is based on a reading of surviving student union records for the period.

56. UCS, *Newsletter*, 15 January 1987; *BP*, 23 January 1987.

57. 'Quiet Goes the Don', *The Spectator*, 21 November 1987.

58. UCS, *Newsletter*, 26 February 1987.

59. *BP*, 10 February 1987.

60. *BP*, 3 February 1987; UCS, *Newsletter*, 26 February 1987.

61. *BP*, 24 February 1987.

Acknowledgements

This book was written in the shadow of two larger projects, although it is quite different in size and scope. My first thanks are to those friends and colleagues who encouraged my research in this field; as they say, they know who they are. Particular thanks are due (in alphabetical order) to Sam Blaxland, Sue Bruley, Alun Burge, Tony Collins, Matt Cook, Jonathan Davies, Victoria Dawson, Rhian Diggins, Dai Donovan, Barry Doyle, Susan Edwards, Hannah Elizabeth, Hywel Francis, Emyr Gruffydd, Tom Hulme, Alex Jackson, Sian James, LGSM, Rhian Keyse, Patrick McDonagh, Jack McLean, Mike Parker, Ben Roberts, Michael Ryan, David Selway, George Severs, Norena Shopland, Dai Smith, Evan Smith, Meic Stephens, Rachel Sweet, Steve Thompson, David Toms, Peter Wakelin, Stephanie Ward, Christian Webb, Llion Wigley, Martin Wright and Luke Young. Tim Foskett shared his memories of 1980s Cardiff with me which transformed the later sections.

Following the release of *Pride* in 2014, I began to ask myself whether, despite the obvious fictional licence taken with aspects of the original story, circumstances in the Dulais valley were unique or were more typical than has been supposed. What, if anything, I asked myself did the story tell us about the social and cultural atmosphere of those supposed socially conservative valley communities. My first foray into this field was thus entirely in keeping with my work as a labour historian. It did not last. Travelling further back in time and reading sources with which I had long been familiar in a different light meant learning a new language to use in the archives and a willingness to dispose of mutual embarrassment when archivists opened a box of pamphlets with covers more risqué than those normally produced in the search room. For their assistance, guidance, and encouragement, I am especially grateful to the Bishopsgate Institute, Bristol Archives, the British Library, the Labour History Archive and Study Centre, the LSE Archives, Sheffield Archives and Local Studies, the West Glamorgan Archives and the Working Class Movement Library.

As always, the support I have received from archives closer to home has been second to none. Much of the early research for the book was carried out at Cardiff University's Special Collections and Archives. Special thanks to everyone for fielding seemingly endless requests for boxes of student newspapers and other records and for sharing in the brainstorming about where to go next. Staff at the Richard Burton Archives and the South Wales Miners' Library were similarly patient and accommodating. The support given by the Glamorgan Archives has been enormous and this book really would not exist without it – the staff there have walked miles to fetch records and have spent many hours discussing many aspects of this research. One result of our mutual endeavour was a guide to LGBT resources written by Norena Shopland and myself. This book is another. I owe Susan Edwards and Rhian Diggins an additional debt of gratitude for allowing me to navigate records freely and for guidance in the use of records not normally the territory of a nineteenth-and twentieth-century historian.

Few research projects have been as personal as this one. My childhood and adolescence coincided almost exactly with the implementation and enforcement of Section 28. Introduced in 1988 when I was a toddler, it was abolished in 2003 when I was in my final year of Sixth Form. Its legacy was still palpable when I went up to Oxford in the autumn of 2004. Talking to friends and former teachers in more recent times, it is clear just how fundamentally the legislation marked – and continues to mark – those of us who went to school during the period of its existence. To be blunt: this is a book that should have been written a long time ago. In many ways, Section 28 left an entire generation in search of lost time and I owe it to those friends who listened and pointed me in the right direction. But especially to Rhian Keyse, David Toms and Christian Webb. Whether a dedication quite pays off the debt, I do not know, but I offer it all the same. This book is for you.

Select Bibliography

ARCHIVAL SOURCES

Bishopsgate Institute, London
Lesbian and Gay News Media Archive

Bristol Archives
Bristol South/South East Constituency Labour Party Records
Charles Beaton Papers

Cardiff Local Studies and Heritage Library, Cathays
Bro Taf HIV/AIDS Review
Cardiff AIDS Helpline, Annual Reports
Cardiff Body Positive, *Time to Care*
Cardiff City Police, Annual Reports of the Chief Constable
Cardiff Community Health Council, Annual Reports

Glamorgan Archives, Cardiff
Cardiff Borough/City Police Records
Cardiff Borough Petty Sessions Records
Cardiff Prison Records
Cardiff Women's Centre Records
Carinwen Morgan Collection
Caroline Joll Collection
FRIEND South Wales Records

Glamorgan Constabulary Records
Merthyr Tydfil Borough Police Records
Merthyr Tydfil Petty Sessions Records
Mid Glamorgan Health Authority Records
Older Lesbian Network (Wales) Records
Ray T. Davies Papers
South Glamorgan Health Authority Records
South Wales Police Records
South Wales Women's Support Group Records

Labour History Archive and Study Centre, Manchester
Communist Party of Great Britain Records
Labour Party Records
Lesbian and Gays Support the Miners Records

London School of Economics, Archives
Campaign for Homosexual Equality Records, including CHE
    Cardiff, *Newsletter*
Friend Records
Gay Liberation Front Records
Peter Tatchell Papers

National Library of Wales, Aberystwyth
Labour Party Wales Records
Leo Abse Papers
MS 23106 E 13
MS ex 2827, Sgript *Bydd yn Wrol*
Plaid Cymru Records

National Screen and Sound Archive of Wales, Aberystwyth
HTV Wales Archive

Richard Burton Archives, Swansea University
Neath, Dulais and Swansea Valleys Miners' Support Group
    Records
Swansea University Student Union Records

South Wales Miners' Library, Swansea
AUD/328: Interview with Tom Davies
AUD/504: Interview with Sian James and Margaret Donovan
AUD/507: Interview with Hefina Headon and Chistine Powell
AUD/509: Interview with Christine Powell
AUD/510: Interview with Hefina Headon
AUD/515: Interview with Ali Thomas
AUD/547: Interview with David Donovan
AUD/583: Interview with Neath, Dulais and Ystalyfera Women's
    Support Group

Special Collections and Archives, Cardiff University
Cardiff Trades Council Records
South Glamorgan Health Authority Annual Reports
University College Cardiff Student Handbooks

The National Archives, Kew, London
Cabinet Papers
Home Office Papers

University of South Wales Archives, Treforest
Polytechnic of Wales Student Handbooks
Polytechnic of Wales Student Newspapers

West Glamorgan Archives, Swansea
Jenny Lynn Papers
South Wales Evening Post Cuttings Files
Swansea Gaol Records
Swansea Women's Centre Records
Ursula Masson Papers

NEWSPAPERS AND PERIODICALS
Aberdare Leader
Athenaeum, The
Bad Press
Body Politic (Toronto)

Broadsheet (Cardiff)
Broadsheet (Leeds)
Cambrian, The
Capital Gay
Cardiff People's Paper
Cardiff Times
Daily Express
Daily Mail
Daily Mirror
Daily Telegraph
Ddraig Binc, Y
Double Take
Evening Express
Evening Leader/Wrexham Evening Leader
Gair Rhydd
Gay Left
Gay News
Gay Noise
Gay Times
Guardian, The
International Times
Lampeter Grapevine
Lesbian and Gay Socialist
Mail on Sunday
Marxism Today
Merthyr Express
Morning Star
News of the World
Observer, The
Pink Paper
Pontypridd Observer
Red Mole
Rhondda Leader
Seren (Bangor)
Socialist Woman
South Wales Argus

South Wales Daily News
South Wales Daily Post
South Wales Echo
South Wales Evening Post
South Wales Weekly Post
Spare Rib
Spectator, The
Square Peg
The Stage
Times, The
Union Eyes
University College Swansea Newsletter
Valleys Star
The Vote
Welsh Nation
Western Mail

PRINTED PRIMARY SOURCES

Abse, Leo, *Private Member* (London, 1973)

Booth, Cath, *Out at Work: Campaigning for Lesbian and Gay Rights* (London, 1989)

Burston, Paul, *Queen's Country* (London, 2008)

Coles, Richard, *Fathomless Riches: Or How I Went from Pop to Pulpit* (London, 2014)

Davies, Ray, *A Miner's Life* (Caerphilly, 2013)

Davies, Rhys, *A Print of the Hare's Foot* (Bridgend, 1997 edn)

Health Promotion Authority for Wales, *Strategic Directions for the Health Promotion Authority for Wales* (Cardiff, 1990)

Jenkins, Roy, *The Labour Case* (London, 1959)

Jenkins, Roy, *Life at the Centre: Memoirs of a Radical Reformer* (London, 1991)

Labour Research Department, *Solidarity with the Miners* (London, 1985)

Morris, Jan, *Conundrum* (London, 1974)

O'Grady, Paul, *Still Standing: My Savage Years* (London, 2012)

Welsh AIDS Campaign, *AIDS: What It Means For Young People* (Cardiff, 1987)

Wildeblood, Peter, *Against the Law* (London, 1955)

SECONDARY SOURCES

Aaron, Jane (ed.), *Our Sisters' Land* (Cardiff, 1994)

Baker, Roger, *Drag: A History of Female Impersonation in the Performing Arts* (New York, 1995)

Beddoe, Deirdre, *Discovering Women's History: A Practical Guide to Researching the Lives of Women since 1800* (London, 1998)

Beddoe, Deirdre, *Out of the Shadows: A History of Women in Twentieth-century Wales* (Cardiff, 2000)

Bell, David and Gill Valentine, 'Queer Country: Rural Lesbian and Gay Lives', *Journal of Rural Studies*, 11/2 (1995), 113–122

Bengry, Justin, 'Profit (f)or the Public Good? Sensationalism, Homosexuality, and the Postwar Popular Press', *Media History*, 20/2 (2014), 146–66

Berridge, Virginia, *AIDS in the UK: The Making of a Policy, 1981–1994* (Oxford, 1996)

Berry, David, *Wales and the Cinema: The First Hundred Years* (Cardiff, 1994)

Betteridge, Tom (ed.), *Sodomy in Early Modern Europe* (Manchester, 2002)

Black, Lawrence, 'Making Britain a Gayer and More Cultivated Country: Wilson, Lee, and the Creative Industries in the 1960s', *Contemporary British History*, 20/3 (2006)

Blakey, V., R. Parish and D. Reid, 'Health promotion responses to AIDS in Wales: the Welsh AIDS campaign', in Maryan Pye, Mukesh Kapila, Graham Buckley and Deirdre Cunningham (eds), *Responding to the AIDS Challenge: A Comparative Study of Local AIDS Programmes in the United Kingdom* (London, 1989)

Blaxland, Sam, 'Denbigh Constituency's First and Final Conservative MP: A Study of Geraint Morgan', *Transactions of the Denbighshire Historical Society*, 65 (2017), 87–100.

Bloch, Michael, *Jeremy Thorpe* (London, 2014)

Bray, Alan, 'Homosexuality and the Signs of Male Friendship in Elizabethan England', *History Workshop*, 29 (1990)

Bray, Alan, *Homosexuality in Renaissance England* (London, 1982)

Cameron, Ross, 'Images of Tiger Bay, 1845–1970', *Patterns of Prejudice*, 31/2 (1997)

Clarke, Anna, *Desire: A History of European Sexuality* (London, 2008)

Cocks, H. G., *Nameless Offences: Homosexual Desire in the Nineteenth Century* (London, 2003)

Cocks, H. G., *Classified: The Secret History of the Personal Column* (London, 2009)

Cocks, Harry, 'Safeguarding Civility: Sodomy, Class and Moral Reform in Early Nineteenth Century England', *Past & Present*, 190/1 (2006), 121–146

Cook, Matt, 'AIDS, Mass Observation, and the Fate of the Permissive Turn', *Journal of the History of Sexuality*, 26/2 (2017), 239–272

Cook, Matt, '"Archives of Feeling": The AIDS Crisis in Britain, 1987', *History Workshop Journal*, 83/1 (2017), 51–78

Cook, Matt, *London and the Culture of Homosexuality, 1885–1914* (Cambridge, 2003)

Cook, Matt, *Queer Domesticities: Homosexuality and Home Life in Twentieth-century London* (London, 2014)

Cook, Matt, Robert Mills, Randolph Trumbach and H. G. Cocks, *A Gay History of Britain: Love and Sex Between Men since the Middle Ages* (London, 2007)

Coxon, A. P. M., *Between the Sheets: Sexual Diaries and Gay Men's Sex in the Era of AIDS* (London, 1996)

Cross, William, *The Abergavenny Witch Hunt* (Abergavenny, 2014)

Davidson, Roger and Gayle Davis, '"A Field for Private Members": The Wolfenden Committee and Scottish Homosexual Law Reform, 1950–1967', *Twentieth Century British History*, 15/2 (2004)

Davies, Miranda and Natania Jansz, *Women Travel: Adventures, Advice and Experience* (London, 1994)

Davies, Peter M., Ford C. I. Hickson, Peter Weatherburn and Andrew J. Hunt, *Sex, Gay Men and AIDS* (London, 1993)

Doan, Laura, *Fashioning Sapphism: The Origins of Modern Lesbian Culture* (New York, 2001)

Evans, David Trevor, *Sexual Citizenship: The Material Construction of Sexualities* (London, 1993)

Francis, Hywel, *History On Our Side* (London, 2015 edn)

Gleeson, Kate, 'Freudian Slips and Coteries of Vice: The Sexual Offences Act of 1967', *Parliamentary History*, 27/3 (2008), 393–409

Gowing, Laura, Michael Hunter and Miri Rubin (eds), *Love, Friendship and Faith in Europe, 1300–1800* (London, 2006)

Gramich, Katie (ed.), *The Works of Gwerful Mechain* (London, 2018)

Grey, Antony, *Speaking Out: Writings on Sex, Law, Politics and Society, 1954–95* (London, 1997)

Griffiths, Colin, Elizabeth Cruse, Joan Harries, Toni Williams, and B. N. C. Littlepage, 'AIDS – A Health Education Approach in West Glamorgan', *Health Education Journal*, 44/4 (1985)

Hall-Carpenter Archives, *Walking after Midnight: Gay Men's Life Stories* (London, 1989)

Harries, Leslie, *Barddoniaeth Huw Cae Llwyd, Ieuan ap Huw Cae Llwyd, Ieuan Dyfi, a Gwerful Mechain* (unpublished MA thesis, Swansea, 1933)

Helmholz, R. H., *The Canon Law and Ecclesiastical Jurisdiction from 597 to the 1640s* (Oxford, 1987)

Herzog, Dagmar, *Sexuality in Europe: A Twentieth-century History* (London, 2011)

Higgins, Patrick, *Heterosexual Dictatorship: Male Homosexuality in Postwar Britain* (London, 1996)

Hitchcock, Tim, 'The Reformulation of Sexual Knowledge in Eighteenth-century England', *Signs: Journal of Women in Culture and Society*, 37/4 (2012)

Holden, Katherine, *The Shadow of Marriage: Singleness in England, 1914–60* (Manchester, 2007)

Houlbrook, Matt, *Queer London: Perils and Pleasures in the Sexual Metropolis, 1918–1957* (Chicago, 2005)

Houlbrook, Matt, 'The Man with the Powderpuff in Interwar London', *The Historical Journal*, 50/1 (2007), 145–171

Houlbrook, Matt and H. G. Cocks (eds), *Palgrave Advances in the Modern History of Sexuality* (London, 2006)

Houlbrook, Matt and Chris Waters, 'The Heart in Exile: Detachment and Desire in 1950s London', *History Workshop Journal*, 62/1 (2006), 142–165

Hurcombe, Linda (ed.), *Sex and God* (London, 1987)

Ingram, Martin, 'Sexual Manners: The Other Face of Civility in Early Modern England', in Peter Burke, Brian Harrison and Paul Slack (eds), *Civil Histories: Essays Presented to Sir Keith Thomas* (Oxford, 2000)

Ingram, Martin, *Carnal Knowledge: Regulating Sex in England, 1470–1600* (Cambridge, 2017)

Ingram, Martin, *Church Courts, Sex, and Marriage in England, 1570–1640* (London, 1987)

Jackson, Louise A., *Women Police: Gender, Welfare and Surveillance in the Twentieth Century* (Manchester, 2006)

James, Dafydd, 'Y Queer Yn Erbyn Y Byd', *Taliesin*, 151 (2014), 81

James, Dafydd, *Llwyth* (Aberystwyth, 2010)

John, Angela V. (ed.), *Our Mothers' Land: Chapters in Welsh Women's History, 1830–1939* (Cardiff, 2011 edn)

John, Angela V., *Rocking the Boat: Welsh Women Who Championed Equality, 1840–1939* (Cardigan, 2018)

John, Angela V., *Turning the Tide: The Life of Lady Rhondda* (Cardigan, 2013)

Johnston, Dafydd (ed.), *Medieval Welsh Erotic Poetry* (Bridgend, 1998)

Jones, David J. V., *Crime and Policing in the Twentieth Century: The South Wales Experience* (Cardiff, 1996)

Jones, David J. V., *Crime in Nineteenth-century Wales* (Cardiff, 1992)

Ledger, Sally, *The New Woman: Fiction and Feminism at the Fin de Siècle* (Manchester, 1997)

Leeworthy, Daryl, 'For Our Common Cause: Sexuality and Left Politics in South Wales, 1967–1985', *Contemporary British History*, 30/2 (2016), 260–280

Leeworthy, Daryl, 'Hidden From View? Male Homosexuality in Twentieth-Century Wales', *Llafur* (2015), 97–119

Leeworthy, Daryl, *Labour Country: Political Radicalism and Social Democracy in South Wales, 1831–1985* (Cardigan, 2018)

Lewis, Brian (ed.), *British Queer History: New Approaches and Perspectives* (Manchester, 2013)

Lewis, Brian, *Wolfenden's Witnesses: Homosexuality in Postwar Britain* (London, 2016)

Linkinen, Tom, *Same-Sex Sexuality in Late Medieval English Culture* (Amsterdam, 2015)

McSheffrey, Shannon, *Marriage, Sex, and Civic Culture in Medieval London* (Philadelphia, 2006)

Medhurst, Jamie, *A History of Independent Television in Wales* (Cardiff, 2010)

Milne, Ida, *Stacking the Coffins: Influenza, War and Revolution in Ireland, 1918–19* (Manchester, 2018)

Mort, Frank, *Capital Affairs: London and the Making of the Permissive Society* (New Haven, 2010)

Muir, Angela Joy, 'Courtship, Sex and Poverty: Illegitimacy in Eighteenth-Century Wales', *Social History*, 43/1 (2018), 56–80

Nobbs, M., 'Queer and Welsh: Double the Trouble', *Rouge* 16, (1994)

Nutbeam, Don, John C. Catford, Simon A. Smail and Colin Griffiths, 'Public Knowledge and Attitudes to AIDS', *Public Health* 103 (1989), 205–11.

Osborne, Huw (ed.), *Queer Wales: The History, Culture and Politics of Queer Life in Wales* (Cardiff, 2016)

Osborne, Huw, *Rhys Davies* (Cardiff, 2009)

Outhwaite, R. B., *The Rise and Fall of the English Ecclesiastical Courts, 1500–1860* (Cambridge, 2007)

Parker, Mike, 'Polls apart', in John Osmond and Peter Finch (eds), *25/25 Vision: Welsh Horizons Across 50 Years* (Cardiff, 2012)

Poole, Steve, '"Bringing great shame upon this city": Sodomy, the Courts, and the Civic Idiom in Eighteenth-century Bristol', *Urban History*, 34/1 (2007)

Porter, Kevin and Jeffrey Weeks, *Between the Acts: Lives of Homosexual Men, 1885–1967* (London, 1991)

Roberts, C., V. Blakey and C. Smith 'Changes in Public Knowledge and Attitudes to HIV/AIDS in Wales, 1987 to 1992', *AIDS Care* 6/4 (1994)

Robinson, Lucy, *Gay Men and the Left in Post-war Britain: How the Personal Got Political* (Manchester, 2007)

Seddon, Vicky (ed.), *The Cutting Edge: Women and the Pit Strike* (London, 1986)

Severs, George J., 'The "Obnoxious Mobilised Minority": Homophobia and Homohysteria in the British National Party, 1982–1999', *Gender and Education* 29/2 (2017), 165–81

Shopland, Norena, *Forbidden Lives: LGBT Histories from Wales* (Bridgend, 2017)

Smith, Bruce R., *Homosexual Desire in Shakespeare's England: A Cultural Poetics* (Chicago, 1991)

Smith, Dai, *Out of the People: A Century in Labour* (Aberystwyth, 2001)

Smith, Evan and Daryl Leeworthy, 'Before *Pride*: The Struggle for the Recognition of Gay Rights in the British Communist Movement, 1973–85', *Twentieth Century British History*, 27/4 (2016), 621–42

Smith, Helen, *Masculinity, Class and Same-Sex Desire in Industrial England, 1895–1957* (London, 2015)

Stephens, Meic, *Rhys Davies: A Writer's Life* (Cardigan, 2013)

Suggett, Richard, 'Slander in Early Modern Wales', *Bulletin of the Board of Celtic Studies*, 39 (1992), 119–53

Tate, Tim with LGSM, *Pride: The Unlikely Story of the Unsung Heroes of the Miners' Strike* (London, 2017)

Thomas, M. Wynn, '"Never Seek to Tell Thy Love": Rhys Davies's Fiction', *Welsh Writing in English*, 4 (1998), 1–21

Van Gelder, Lindsy and Pamela Robin Brandt, *Are You Two ... Together? A Gay and Lesbian Travel Guide to Europe* (London, 1991)

Van Morgan, S. A., 'Plaid Cymru – The Party of Wales: the new politics of Welsh nationalism at the dawn of the 21st century', in L. De Winter, M. Gomez-Reino and P. Lynch (eds), *Autonomist Parties in Europe: Identity Politics and the Revival of the Territorial Cleavage* (Barcelona, 2006)

Waites, Matthew, *The Age of Consent: Young People, Sexuality and Citizenship* (London, 2005)

Weeks, Jeffrey, *Coming Out: Homosexual Politics in Britain from the Nineteenth Century to the Present* (London, 1977)

Weeks, Jeffrey, *The World We Have Won* (London, 2007)

Williams, John, *Bloody Valentine: A Killing in Cardiff* (London, 1995)

Index

A

Abercynon xiv
Aberdare
    Gay Liberation Front in 103
Abergwynfi 3
    Caersalem Baptist Chapel in 3
Abertillery 91
Aberystwyth xxix(n), 8–9, 43
    Cottaging in 51
    Gay Bars in 71
    Gay Liberation Front in 103
    Section 28 Protests in 126
Abraham, Annis 75–6
Abse, Leo xxii, xxiii, xxv, xxvii, 37, 91,
        93, 106
    Appearance on *We Who Have
        Friends* (1969) xxiv, xxv
    Sexual Offences Bill (1961) xxiii
    Sexual Offences Act (1967) xxiv,
        xxv
    Speaking on the BBC xxiii, xxiv,
        93
    Views on bisexuality 106–7
    Views on transgender 106
Activism xvii, 54, 60, 95, 98–104
Afan Valley 3
AIDS *see* HIV/AIDS
Alderson, Ronald 35
    see also Police
Anderson, Donald (Doctor) 122
Ar Dâf 78
Arfon Borough Council 118

Arran, Earl of xxii
*Artist and Journal of Home Culture,
    The* 46
Ashwell, Lena 4
Athenaeum, The 47
Attlee, Clement 90

B

Balfour, Campbell 75
Bangor
    First All-Wales Gay Rights
        Conference held in 103
    Gay Bars in 71–2
    Gay Liberation Front in 103
    Lesbian Line in 60
    Section 28 Protests in 125
    Women's Centre in 82
    see also University College of
        North Wales, Bangor
Barry 13, 29, 30
Barry Dock News 10
Basini, Mario (Journalist) 52
Bath 104
BBC xxiii, 93, 104, 134(n)
Beddoe, Deirdre (Historian) xxviii
Behaviours
    Bathing 50
    Bed Sharing 12
    Cottaging 50–1, 62
    Cruising 62, 94
    Dancing 67–8

Behaviours (CONTINUED)
  Drag 6, 7, 9–10, 67
  Friendship 12
  Intimacy 12
  Kissing 12
  Masturbation 12, 50
  Nudity 48–9
  Promiscuity 61
  Same-Sex Desire 12, 16, 23–4
  Sex 13, 16, 23, 49
Berridge, Virginia (Historian)
      120
Beynon, Ann 104
Birmingham 104
Bisexuality, relative absence in
      historical record xxvii
Blaengwynfi 6
Bob yn y Ddinas 76–7
  see also Eirian, Siôn
Body Politic (Toronto) 44
Bookshops 82
    Gay's the Word 97
    in Cardiff 82
    in Machynlleth 54, 82
    in Swansea 82
Borrow, George 47
Bowen, Roderick 91
Bristol 8, 16, 104
British Broadcasting Corporation
    see BBC
British Medical Association xxv
Broughton, Phyllis 9
Buggery *see* Behaviours; Sex
Burston, Paul 78
Bydd yn Wrol xvi

C
Cadoxton 23
Campaign for Homosexual Equality
      54, 60, 95
    in Cardiff 98–9, 103–4
    in Gwynedd 98
    in Newport 103–7
    Relationship with the Labour
      Party 98, 105
    Relationship with Plaid Cymru
      98

    Women's Group in Cardiff
      99–100
    Women in 100–1
Campaign for Nuclear Disarmament
      55
Cardiff xiv, xx, xxiii, xxix(n), 18, 28–33,
      44, 48, 53, 57, 68, 82, 110
    AIDS Helpline in 121–2
    Campaign for Homosexual
      Equality in 98–9, 103–4
    Erotica in 48
    Gay Bars in 62–3, 68, 70, 74–83,
      104
    Gay Liberation Front in 101–3,
      109
    Lesbian Line in 60, 65(n)
    Library subscriptions in 46–7
    LGSM Group in xiv
    Museum and Art Gallery 46–7
    Rights and Information Bureau
      62, 82, 102
    see also University College
      Cardiff
Cardiff People's Paper 102
Cardiff Trades Council 125
Carpenter, Edward 69
Cashman, Michael 124
Chapter Arts Centre 98–9, 104
CHE *see* Campaign for Homosexual
      Equality
Cheltenham 104
Chester 72
Church in Wales 125
Classified Advertising 43–6
    Coded 44–5
    Lonely Hearts Columns 43–4,
      45–6
    Rural advertisers compared with
      urban advertisers 44
Clwyd County Council 108
Codner, Daniel John Drew 26–8
Coff, Peter 79
Colwyn Bay 54
Coming Out 57–63
Communist Party (of Great Britain)
      97
Consent, Age of xxv, xxvi, 107
Conservative Family Campaign 123

Conservative Party xxvi, 37, 91, 105
    Homophobia in 111(n), 123, 127
Cook, Matt (Historian) 57
Counties (Traditional)
    Anglesey 16–17
    Breconshire 17
    Cardiganshire (Ceredigion)
      16–17, 50
    Caernarfonshire 16–17
    Carmarthenshire 16–17, 43, 50
    Denbighshire 16–17
    Flintshire 17
    Glamorgan 17
    Meirionnydd 16–17
    Montgomeryshire 16–17
    Monmouthshire 17
    Pembrokeshire 17, 26
    Radnorshire 16–17
Courts 16–19, 24–5
    Assize Courts 18, 27, 28
    of Great Session 16, 17
    Indictments in 16–17
    and Racism 28–30
Criccieth xix
Currie, Edwina 107
CYLCH xxix(n)

D
Dafydd xvi, xvii
Daily Herald 90
Daily Mirror 89
Davies, Alun 124
Davies, Clement 91
Davies, Elfed 91
Davies, Ray (Councillor) 96
Davies, Rhys 11–12, 69
Davies, S. O. (Stephen Owen) 74, 91
Davies, Tom 3–8, 11–12, 19
    in France, 4
    as Peggy Deauville 5, 6
Dillwyn, (Elizabeth) Amy xxvi
Donnelly, Desmond 90–1, 128
Donovan, Dai xii, xiii
Dowlais 49, 52
Drag 3–11, 19
Dulais Valley xi, xiii, 125
Dyson, Tony 90

E
Edwards, Ness 91
Eirian, Siôn xv, 76–7
Emlyn, Endaf xv
Erotica 48
Escamilla, José 28
Evening Express 10, 44

F
Family Planning Association 123
Female Impersonation *see* Drag
Foot, Michael 106
Foskett, Tim 79–81, 104, 120, 126
    Organises First Gay Pride March
      in Cardiff 109–10
    Wales Against Clause 28
      Co-ordinator 124, 125
First World War 3, 7, 45
    Concert Parties in 4, 5
    see also Davies, Tom
Flynn, Paul
    Support for Gay Rights 105
    Campaign for Homosexual
      Equality view of 107
Francis, Hywel
    Expresses support for anti-
      Section 28 Campaign 125
FRIEND
    in Cardiff 60–3, 76, 77, 79, 110
    in north Wales 65(n)

G
Gadael Lenin xv, xvi
Gair Rhydd 59–60, 79–81, 125
Gardner, Edward 93
Gay Bars and Clubs 67–8
    in Aberystwyth 71
    in Bangor 71–2
    in Barry 71
    in Caernarfon 71
    in Cardiff 62–3, 68, 70, 74–83,
      104
    in Ferndale 71
    in Llandudno 71
    in Llandrindod Wells 71
    in Merthyr Tydfil 71, 103

Gay Bars and Clubs (CONTINUED)
  in Neath 72
  in Newport 70–1
  in Rhyl 71
  in Swansea 72–4
Gay Beach (Jersey Marine) 50
Gay Labour Group 96–97
  see also Labour Campaign for
      Lesbian and Gay Rights
Gay Liberation Front 57, 94, 95,
      101–3
  in Aberdare 103
  in Aberystwyth 103
  in Bangor 103
  in Cardiff 101–3, 109
  in Swansea 103
Gay men
  Dominance of in historical
      records xxvi–xxvii
Gay News 44, 82
Gay Pride *see* Pride March
Gay Rights *see* LGBT Rights
Gay Rural Aid and Information
      Network 54–5
  Influence of *The Good Life* on 55
Gay Sweatshop
  Poppies performed in Swansea
      116
Glyncorrwg 3, 6, 7,
Gordon Coffee Tavern (Cardiff) 69
Gore, Arthur *see* Arran, Earl of
GRAIN *see* Gay Rural Aid and
      Information Network
Griffiths, Colin (Doctor) 118–19
Guardian, The 89
Gwilym, Dafydd ap 15
Gwynedd County Council 108

H
Hall, Radclyffe 10
Harrington, Richard xvi
Haverfordwest 17
Headon, Hefina xiii
Hellenism 47
Homoeroticism 46–7
Homosexual Law Reform Society 90
Horsfall, Allan 95–6

House of Commons xxiii, 91–3
House of Lords xxiii
Housing 44–5, 94
  Squatting 57
HIV/AIDS xv, xix, 79, 115–16, 121–4
  Education resources 118
  Helplines 121–2
  Support Services 122
  Response in Gwent 121–2
  Response in South Glamorgan
      115, 121–2
  Response in West Glamorgan
      118–19, 121
  see also Welsh AIDS Campaign
Hughes, Emrys 91
Hughes, Roy 107

I
Identity
  Class xxvi–xxviii, 6, 23–4
  Effeminacy 43–4
  Gender xxvi, 9, 26, 33–5
  Masculinity 11, 26
  Race xxvi, 28–33
  see also Welshness
Ingram, Martin (Historian) 14
International Times 44

J
Jackson, Charles Kains 46–7
Jackson, Mike xi, 125
  see also Lesbians and Gays
      Support the Miners
James, Dafydd 82–3
James, Siân xi
Jenkins, Roy xxii, xxv, 37, 90
  Labour Case, The 40(n)
Jersey Marine
  Gay beach at 50
John, Brynmor 123
Jones, David (Historian) 17–18
Josephson, Mimi 88

K
King, Hetty 9

Kinnock, Neil
    Support for Equalisation of
        Consent 128
    Views on homosexuality 107

L
Labouchère Amendment (1885) 18
Labouchère, Henry 18
Labour Campaign for Lesbian and
        Gay Rights
    in Wales 97
    see also Gay Labour Group
Labour Party xxii, xxvii, 96, 127
    Attitudes amongst MPs 90–1,
        106–7, 128
    see also Gay Labour Group;
        Labour Campaign for Lesbian
        and Gay Rights
Lampeter, Wimmin's Land 55
Lancaster, Lenny 76, 78
Lee, Jennie xxii
Legislation
    Buggery Act (1533) 13–14
    Criminal Law Amendment Act
        (1885) 18
    Education Act (1993) 127
    Local Government Act (1988)
        124, 126–7
    Matrimonial Clauses Act (1963)
        xxiii
    Sexual Offences Bill (1961) xxiii
    Sexual Offences Act (1967) 93–4
Lesbians
    Appeal of Swansea to 73
    Night club events aimed at 80
    Profiling by Police 25–6
    see also Women's Organisation
Lesbians and Gays Support the
        Miners xi–xiv
    All Out! Dancing in Dulais xiv
    Pits and Perverts (Camden
        Electric Ballroom) xiii
Lesbian Line xxvi, 60
    in Bangor 60
    in Cardiff 60, 65(n)
    in Swansea 60
Lewis, Richard 123, 131–2

LGBT Rights xix, xxv, xxviii, 127–8,
        132
LGSM *see* Lesbians and Gays Support
        the Miners
Liberal Party 18, 91, 124
Liberation
    Gay xiv, xviii, xxviii, 57, 81
    Women's xiii, 55, 60, 82, 100,
        131
Link, The 45–6
Llanddewi Brefi 56
Llandeilo xvii
Llangollen, Ladies of xxvi
Llwyth 82–3
Locations for sex xx, xxi
    Cars 50
    Cinemas 50
    Hillsides 50
    Hotels and Lodging Houses 50
    Parks 51
    Public Transport 50–1
    Swimming baths 49
    Taxis xx, xxi
    Toilets 50–1
    Urinals 18–19
    Workplace 51
London xii, 3, 6, 8, 27
London School of Economics (LSE)
        95

M
Machynlleth
    Centre for Alternative Technology
        54
    Quarry Bookshop 54, 82
Magazine of Art, The 48
Magazines
    Body Politic (Toronto) 44
    Rico-CHE (Newport) 107
Male Impersonation 9
    see also Drag
Manic Street Preachers 80
Marquand, Hilary 91
Marxism Today 44
Mass Observation 67
Mathew, Theobald 88
Mechain, Gwerful 15–16

Merchant Navy 28–31
    Greeks in 30–1
    Maltese in 31
    Muslims in 28–9
Merthyr Tydfil 25, 33, 49, 52–3, 79
    Gar Bars in 71, 103
    see also Pugh, Billy
Methodology xvii–xviii, xxvi, xxvii,
    13–16
    see also Terminology
Meye, Percy 7–8
Morgan, Evan (Viscount Tredegar)
    xxvi
Morris, Islwyn xvi
Morris, Jan
    Conundrum, Leo Abse's views
        on 106

N

National Front 81, 124–5
National Union of Mineworkers
    xiii–xiv, 96
National Union of Students xiii,
    103
    All-Wales Gay Rights Conference
        103–4
National Union of Students Wales
    104
National Vigilance Association 48
Neath, Dulais and Swansea Valleys
    Miners' Support Group xi,
    125
    see also Lesbians and Gays
        Support the Miners
Newport
    Campaign for Homosexual
        Equality in 103–7
    Gay Bars in 70–1
    Gay sauna in 50
    News Chronicle 89
Newsletters
    Rico-CHE (Newport)
New Woman 9–10
    See also Liberation, Women's
Norwich 27
NUM *see* National Union of
    Mineworkers

O

O'Grady, Paul 78
Onllwyn xi, xii
Organisation for Lesbian and Gay
    Action 124
Owens, Nigel 73–4

P

Padley, Walter 91
Paris 5–6
Parker, Mike (Author) 98
Parliament 89–90
    See also House of Commons;
        House of Lords
Peace News 55
Penarth 10, 47
Permissiveness 89
Pink Paper 82
Pirie, George 28
Plaid Cymru 97–8
Police xx, xxi, 88
    Cardiff City xx, xxi, 25, 33, 34, 35
    Glamorgan 35, 36
    Merthyr Tydfil 25, 33, 35
    Metropolitan xxi, 25, 34
    Monmouthshire 35
    Newport 26, 36
    North Wales
    Profiling by 25–6
    Swansea 25, 35
    Women in the 34–5, 39(n)
    see also Courts; *Police Gazette*
Police Gazette 25–6
Polytechnic of Wales 129–30
Pontypool xxiii, 56
Pontypridd
    Conservative Party homophobia
        in 123
    Lesbian-run farm in 56
    Student activism in 129–30
Port Talbot 56
Pride (2014) xi
Pride Cymru 132, 133
Pride March
    in Bristol 108
    in Cardiff 108–9, 120
    in London xiii, 108

Probert, Arthur 91
Pugh, Billy (Merthyr Tydfil) 52–3

Q
Queer Bashing 87

R
Rainbow Flag 81, 130, 132
Rhondda 8, 61, 71, 77
Rhondda Leader 8
Rhymney Valley 61
Rhys, Matthew xvi
Rights and Information Bureau (RIB)
        62, 82, 102
Riordan, Colin 131
Robinson, Kenneth 90
Russell, Bertrand 90

S
Salesbury, William 15
Savage, Lily 78
Scottish Minorities Group 95
Second World War xix, 24, 34, 49, 68
Section 28 116, 129
    Abolition 132
    Implementation in Wales 127
Seren 58
Sexual Offences Act *see* Legislation,
        Sexual Offences Act (1967)
Shopland, Norena (Historian) 110(n)
Sixsmith, Guy 87
Skelhorn, Norman 88
Smith, Chris 124
Smith, Helen (Historian) xix, 36
Social Attitudes
    Gossip xxi
    Homophobia xii–xiii, 11–12, 53–4,
        81, 105, 109, 120, 128
    in British Social Attitudes Survey
        xv–xvi
    in north Wales compared with
        south Wales xix, 107–8
    in south Wales Valleys xii–xiii,
        51–3, 107
    Private behaviour 37

towards HIV/AIDS 120
towards Wolfenden Report 88–9
towards women in male attire
        10–11
Visibility 81–3, 110
Social Democratic Politics xiv, xxvii,
        89
Sodomy *see* Behaviours, Sex
South Glamorgan 115
South Glamorgan Gay Women's
        Group 100
South Wales Echo 9, 44, 76, 109–10
South Wales Valleys xvii, 50–1, 107
South Wales Weekly Post xix
Spanish Flu (1919) 28
Spare Rib 44, 56
Spartacus International Gay Guide 51
Spectator, The 106
Sports Council for Wales 118
Spurrell, W. G. 27
Square Peg xii
St David's Cathedral 27
    see also Codner, Daniel John Drew
St Fagans 88
Steel, David 124
Stonewall Riots (1969) 94–5, 108
Stonewall (Charity) 127
Stonewall Cymru 104, 128, 133
Studio, The 46
Summers, Cyril 105
Support Services *see* HIV/AIDS,
        Helplines; FRIEND; Lesbian
        Line; Rights and Information
        Bureau
Swansea 28, 31–2, 82, 89
    Gay Bars in 72–4
    Gay Liberation Front in 103
    Lesbian Line in 60
Swayne, Desmond 123

T
Tabili, Laura (Historian) 31
Taliesin Theatre, Swansea 116–17
Taslameden, Abdulla 28
Tatchell, Peter 124, 136(n)
Terminology 12, 15–16, 19, 25–6
    see also Methodology

Terrence Higgins Trust 123
Thatcher, Margaret
    Government xv, xxvi, 123–4
    Homophobia of 124
    Introduces Section 28 124
    Supports homosexual law reform
        90
Thomas, George 91
Thomas, Jeffrey 107
Thomas, M. Wynn 131
Thorpe, Jeremy 90
Tiller, John 4
Tilley, Vesta 9
Tonyrefail 50
Transgender 31, 77, 106
    Relative absence in historical
        record xxvii
Treherbert 31

U
Union Eyes 126
University College Cardiff
    Absence of lesbians in GaySoc
        112(n)
    Gay Awareness Week at xiv,
        59–60, 120
    GaySoc at 79
    Showing of *All Out! Dancing in
        Dulais* xiv
    Student Union Bar at 81
University College of North Wales,
    Bangor 58, 103–4
    GaySoc at 58–9
    Lesbian and Gay Awareness Day
        at 125
University College Swansea
    Gay Awareness Week at 130
    GaySoc at 103
    Student Union Campaigns at 130
    Homophobia at 116–18, 130–1
University Hospital of Wales 115
University of South Wales *see*
    Polytechnic of Wales

V
Valleys Star xiii

W
Wales Against Clause 28 124
    March in Cardiff 124–5
Wales TUC supports Wales Against
    Clause 28 Rally 124
Watkins, Cecil Haydn 88
Webster-Gardiner, Graham
Weeks, Jeffrey (Historian) 36
Well of Loneliness, The 10
Welshness xv, 128–9, 132–3
Welsh AIDS Campaign 118–20
    see also HIV/AIDS
Welsh Office 119–20
Welsh Rugby Union 118
We Who Have Friends (1969) xxiv,
    xxv
West, Granville xxiii
Western Mail 44
White, Eirene 89, 91
Wigley, Dafydd 98
Wilde, Oscar 46
Wildeblood, Peter 37
Williams, John (Novelist) 79
Williams, Llywelyn 91–3, 111(n)
Wilson, James Arthur 33–5,
    39(n)
    see also Police
Wimmin's Land 55–6
Windsor, Barbara 78
Wolfenden Committee 37
    Evidence of Association of Chief
        Constables to 88
    Parliamentary Debate on Report
        of 91–3
    Report of (1957) 37, 87–93
Women's Organisation
    Campaign for Homosexual
        Equality Women's Group
        99–101
    Discos 80
    Lesbian Lines 60, 65(n)
    South Glamorgan Gay Women's
        Group 100
    Women's Centres 82, 109

Y
Yellow Book 46